Such a Little Secret

Such a Little Secret

J. Wilson Barrett

SPORTS MEDIA GROUP

All inquiries should be addressed to:
Sports Media Group
An imprint of Ann Arbor Media Group LLC
2500 S. State Street
Ann Arbor, MI 48104

Library of Congress Cataloging in Publication data on file.

ISBN: 1-58726-111-1

Printed and bound at Edwards Brothers, Inc., Ann Arbor, MI

10 9 8 7 6 5 4 3 2 1   2004 2005 2006 2007 2008

"Yes, he has and you know Peter, it's such a little secret."

—Henry Longhurst.

(In an aside to Peter Alliss, BBC Television Broadcast ca. 1976)

With especial thanks to Peter Alliss for his encouragement, kind permission to use "snippets" from his writings and the snatch of conversation with the late Henry Longhurst which was to give rise to the title of the book.

also

To Sidney L. Matthew, P.A., President of I.Q. Press Corp. of Tallahassee, Florida U.S.A. for his courtesy and subsequent help in obtaining permissions to use extracts from American publications.

—J. W. B.

*To my friend Bob, who started it all, and
my wife Kathleen, who put up with it all.*

Contents

Introduction

Eighty years ago, as hickory gave way to steel, interest that has always surrounded the game of golf exploded into mania that has yet to ease its grip on millions of the world's aspiring players prepared to spend a lifetime in search of a better game.

The great players and teachers of that time (and ever since) were destined to see a phenomenal demand completely outstrip the available supply of quality instruction. The result has been that measurable improvement of one's game is now enjoyed by far too few.

By 1930, through the simple process of dividing the number of people actively playing golf by the number of those qualified to play in national championships, it was apparent that the ratio stood at an unbelievable 20,000 to 1, or very close to it.

The master players and teachers of the 1920s and 1930s were products of a golden age of golfing knowledge and instruction. They had enjoyed the benefit of teachers who believed that golf was a simple game, success or failure at which turned upon having knowledge of surprisingly few fundamental truths—three or four things to be hammered in until thoroughly learned. Any advancement thereafter came quite readily through self-teaching and common sense.

Those master players and teachers could see no reason whatsoever for such a deteriorating margin of skills within the game. To their credit they were prepared to say so, writing every bit as much on the reasons why each of the 20,000 duffers found themselves unable to play the game as they did on telling them how to do it properly.

Too late! The horse had bolted. The irresistible urge to swing golf clubs any which way and at every opportunity had descended worldwide. An era had ended. Then, as now, the masters could only gaze upon a world of average players that was totally lacking—not in physical ability—but in knowledge. They saw them as wildly out of touch with the essentials of the correct stroke and, despite a lifetime of scores in the high 90s, making no attempt to learn them.

Today, the ratio may well be 40,000 to 1 and is continuing to rise. The juggernaut of ineffective instruction and/or the inability of players to grasp proper instruction could well be irreversible. Nonetheless the odd voice in the wilderness is still occasionally heard.

It has been more than 40 years since the late great Ben Hogan published his definitive work on the few essential elements that go into the making of a golf swing. In his book Hogan wrote of the distress it caused him to watch "average golfers" at practice:

> ...throwing away their energy to no constructive purpose, doing the same wrong things that they have done for years and will continue to do, without improvement, until they are ninety. (*Five Lessons: The Modern Fundamentals of Golf.* Nicholas Kaye Ltd. 1957)

Former Ryder Cup player and current television golf commentator Peter Alliss has also been unafraid to voice his thoughts on teaching and learning. Pondering upon the condition of the average golfer he wrote: "But what I do not know is why so many are content to play so badly, often playing every week, yet they can be quite dreadful. They have no idea of grip, stance or anything, and seem to make no particular effort to get better." (Peter Alliss. *An Autobiography.* Collins 1981)

Most obvious to any onlooker is the difficulty that

beginners and high handicap golfers have in bringing any kind of positive attitude to their learning of the game. Without any knowledge of exactly what it is that must be learned and without any determination to find out, all practice is futile.

They would do as well practicing the violin lacking all knowledge of music.

In light of today's morass of primary and secondary instruction that clearly has not improved the games of millions, it can do no harm to look once more at the opinions of those earlier masters. To them, good golf was the result of a thorough knowledge of the locus (path) that the clubhead must take in the hitting stroke. They taught simplicity and, when practicing, a profitable concentration upon the three or four essential elements, which then put the clubhead on that locus time after time. In short, the very guts of a correct, powerful, and dependable swing.

The following chapters are the screening of a lifetime's interest in the golf swing with the sophisms, half-truths, and blatant misnomers firmly riddled out. The reader may find little that is wholly original. In all cases, however, where the origin of a particular form of words is known, due credit will be given in the text or in the sources appearing at the end of the book, or both.

To any expert or near-expert player who scores somewhere in the 70s or better, this book may be of no more than passing interest. It is for the struggling beginner and those who seldom, if ever, shoot less than 90 that this book has been written—those millions of average golfers ambitious for improvement that, despite all that they may see, hear, read, and do, never seems to come.

It is hoped that it may offer a change of tack and thus raise, refresh, and, above all, maintain the spirits of those who dream of coming to grips with rebuilding their golf swing.

Note: Reference to male and female and left and right at every juncture became as wearisome to write as it is to read. For that reason alone the attempt was discontinued.

Being fully aware that female golfers and left-handed players may form a fair proportion of any readership, the author offers his sincere apology to any who may be irritated by what he or she may consider to be a lapse of correctness.

1

The Great Divide

In any study of golf nothing is more astonishing than the ratio between the millions who play the game poorly and the few individuals who come to master the techniques required for entering professional events or high-level amateur championships.

The fascination lies not in the few hundred expert players who vie for the top spots, but rather in the relative position of the remainder. The plain fact is that the great bulk of the world's golfers will never break 90 in any round they play—and on courses that have nothing of the degree of difficulty encountered at championship level.

Even though the teaching and learning of the game have always been something of a mystery, it doesn't seem unreasonable to have expected that the information explosion of the 1950s that led to today's limitless supply of instruction material would have long since sent most high handicaps tumbling. At the very least it could have been expected to decrease the ratio between the number of players with plus handicaps and those with handicaps of 10 or higher.

Incredibly it has not. In fact, any thorough examination of handicap ratios will show that they have widened considerably. It seems, therefore, that today's player with a handicap of 20 has no more chance of improvement than his counterpart of 150 years ago who had little in the way of instruction and nothing at all in the way of photography or video to help him.

Since the turn of the twentieth century developments in travel, communications, and the availability of records and statistics from both sides of the Atlantic have provided details of individuals, standards, and numbers from which quite accurate ratios may be taken and compared.

After 1900 the trickle of interest then existing in golf rapidly became a flood. By the roaring twenties successful professional golfers were tapping into an endless demand for instruction. Nor was there any shortage of aspirants requiring the services of also-ran pros who countered the greater market value of their more famous peers with the offer of an endless succession of tips and secrets. They also sold a startling array of bizarre aids, all allegedly designed to assist anyone prepared to pay for a reliable, low-scoring golf swing.

Every type of tuition was available on a no money back, no guarantee basis.

As far back as 1930 Bobby Jones observed that in the United States alone, some 7.5 million people were actively playing golf but, in his opinion, perhaps 1 in 20,000 deserved an expert rating. At the same time Jones estimated that the number of American golfers qualified to play at championship level was roughly 400, one in every 20,000 playing the game or thereabouts. That may have been somewhat wide of the mark. From details of U.S. Championship fields of the period it seems probable that the figure of 400 expert players was optimistically high.

As almost every golfer knows, 1930 was the year that Jones won the "Grand Slam" (victories in the British Open, British Amateur, U.S. Open, and U.S. Amateur). Less generally known is the fact that this tremendous success was achieved at a time when he was saddled with a commitment to write a twice-weekly column on golf for the Bell Syndicate of publishers. His columns were to run for eight years.

These wonderful articles not only provided instruction on the techniques needed to produce correctly struck golf shots, they also offered commonsense advice on other matters pertaining to the game that he considered of equal importance.

In an erudite foreword to Jones's book, *Bobby Jones on Golf* (Cassell & Co. 1968), Charles Price wrote that "there is no more rewarding reading in the whole vast library of golf." We have Ben Crenshaw's word for it that his longtime teacher Harvey Penick also shared this view. Penick believed Jones's book was required reading for anyone who wished to improve his game.

In spite of his contributions to help golfers understand the game, Jones was clearly disappointed that his books and articles were unable to do much for the small circle of friends with whom he played socially.

It irked and puzzled him that his lectures, articles, films, clinics, and countless demonstrations seemed to add so little to the progress of the millions of high handicap players that they were specifically designed to help. In occasional asides he also revealed his doubts about the whole conception of golf instruction as traditionally offered. (Jones's thoughts on this will be examined more thoroughly in following chapters.)

In the 1920s and 1930s, almost all championship golf

was played in North America or Great Britain. Today, of course, the game is played worldwide and the number of active golfers must be astronomical. It could well be as many as 30 million—roughly four times as many as there were playing in America in 1930. It could be many more, but let us say four times.

If the ratio of expert golfers to total numbers playing has simply remained static, by use of Jones's rule of thumb we should see 1,600 golfers rated today as being of championship standard.

Are there so many? Possibly. However, a review of the number of players on the various professional tours around the world leads one to seriously doubt it. Even if there *are* 1,600, it still means that the standard of golf played worldwide has stood still for the past 70 years. If there are less than 1,600 players of sufficient quality to contest the great championships, then it can only mean that fewer have made it through from the amateur ranks, whose standards must have declined.

"But," the skeptic might say, "the standard of play must be compared, too. See how much it has improved since, say, 1935." But has it really, when advances in technology, ballistics, and agronomy are brought into the equation?

"But," says the skeptic, "you are talking about la crème de la crème. They play an entirely different game. Everybody knows that."

But they do not. They play golf just as we do. La crème de la crème of golf range from six- foot-six-inch, sixteen-stone giants, to five-foot-nothing, eight-stone weaklings, just as they do in golf clubs. From 19-year-old rookies, to 50-year-old grandfathers, just as they do in golf clubs.

Great championships are most often won by men and women in rudest good health. They have also been won by the halt and the lame, by the old, and occasionally by the downright ill. Yet only one player in 40,000 or more can make it through to such a level. Why? There simply has to be a reason.

"But," says the skeptic, "I still say you're off the planet. If you're looking for improving standards of play, then look to the grass roots. That is where you'll find improvement."

Okay, let's take a look. Let us see whether more courses, practice ranges, teachers, instructional literature, videos, and technological advancement have pulled an encouraging percentage of handicaps down as they might reasonably have been expected to do. Can we agree on a handicap of 10 as being a sensible target for the fit, enthusiastic, and ambitious members prepared to spend time and money to get there?

Alas, at clubs where our skeptic expected encouraging improvement, handicap levels remain much as they were. Disappointingly, other clubs agree that despite much improved facilities handicap levels have gone up not down. Many, in fact, report that a comparison of handicaps over the last 50 years indicates a considerable fall in the standard of play of their current membership.

It is true that certain clubs tend to attract the better players, but even here the average of handicaps shows little or no reduction.

For the majority of golf clubs worldwide, the figures on the handicap sheets tell a dismal story. Clubs with 500 or 600 playing members can be seen to have fewer than 20 playing to a handicap of five or less. (Many have fewer than 10.) Widen this to take in handicaps of nine or less—the rightly admired single digit players—and the ratio to total membership remains desperately poor.

Any comparison of handicaps of 50 years ago may, of course, be clouded by the various changes in the handicapping systems made throughout the period, leaving us with the one in universal use today. It is frequently alleged that 50 years ago the Old Pals Handicap Network was much more loose and friendly, but is that really true?

Oldsters point out (with much justification) that in their day they lacked many of the advantages we have now—advantages that surely should promote better scoring and subsequently lower handicaps.

The range of wonderful machinery available to the greenkeeper/course manager. Every stalk of rough now cut, lessening the possibility of penalty strokes for loss of ball with the added bonus of a simple recovery from all but the wildest of shots. Billiard table greens are commonplace with a hullabaloo if a single one is found to be the least bit furry. Leaves are scooped away by guzzlers even as they fall.

Ancient members will tell you that 60 years ago scores were equally as good as those being returned today. They talk not just of the winning scores, but those right through a competition entry list—scores made, more often than not, within three hours of play and using straightforward equipment. They add that 50 years ago much of today's modern design and technology may well have been considered to be outside the Rules of Golf.

However all this may be, it can be seen at many layouts largely unchanged since 1950 that the card in the clubhouse displaying the course record will be of a surprisingly early date.

To write 10 words on golf is to feel one is walking

on eggs. So all-embracing is the information we already have that it can seem quite impossible to produce a single original thought on the subject. Nonetheless, vast though the library is, it seems to do little for the majority of those that play.

There is general agreement that a huge divide exists (and that it is getting wider) but the difficulties in teaching and learning seem very real. Despite the mass of instruction and facilities available to any enthusiast new to the game, for some obscure reason the odds against him ever playing down to better than five seem impossibly long. Just how long has already been demonstrated. The purpose therefore is to suggest to the pupil, novice, and all experienced players unable to escape from middle and high handicaps, a complete change of tack. In golf as in other things, there will always be those of greater and lesser ability. But it is surely time to take a serious look at whether it really needs to be by such a margin.

What follows is not for golfers within the spread of plus four to a handicap of five. They have arrived within that spread by close study of the fundamentals of the game, followed by intense application and the acquisition of a deep knowledge of "how to learn" for oneself. Few, if any, could tell their best friend—who might well be younger, stronger, and generally sharper—exactly or even remotely how it is done. This has been a difficulty for both teacher and pupil down the ages.

They have probably taken lessons in the fundamentals from just one or more tutors and may have gleaned something from each. Up to a point they may have benefited from the mass of literary and visual instruction that comes in from all directions, but only up to a point.

Somewhere in their progress, be it early or late, realization has dawned that they have learned "how to learn" and the developing expert player, often unawares, splits from being professionally taught to being self-taught. All further advancement is thus firmly in his own hands.

It is this mystical moment of division that Tommy Armour and many other great teachers recognized and understood so well, yet found and still find so difficult to describe. This subtle shift to a kind of self-teaching nirvana all must find if they are ever to progress from five to scratch to plus.

Before this division occurs, the player may be quite unsure of any particular idea or notion of which he is able to say: "That was the moment that opened my eyes and set me on my way."

Even after the transition when he has gone on to join the ranks of the elite, he is as unable as most experts before him to describe his understanding of what constitutes a correctly executed stroke clearly enough to be of much assistance to a newcomer to the game.

Thus we can safely leave all golfers who play to a level of which the duffer can only dream and look more closely at the remainder who, though always hopeful of improvement, play their golf in a progressively lesser category of knowledge and subsequently of skill.

Those with handicaps of six to nine are close to that upper level. Many of these will have already discovered "how to learn" and with further effort will leave the handicap categories at which this book is directed.

Those with handicaps of 10 to 18 have every right to feel that just one spark is all that is required to drive them down to single figures. Alas, most will find that such a spark can prove difficult to ignite. They should read on. There might just be something here to help them.

There remains worldwide the vast majority of all who play golf—the millions who quite simply do not know that they do not know. They too should read on for they have nothing to lose but their ineffective golf swings. Possibly for years an unfailing keenness to improve and a willingness to make considerable expenditure on every kind of instruction and the very best in equipment, has been followed by endless futile practice and hundreds of rounds of play, none of which has cut a single stroke from a handicap remaining stubbornly in the middle 20s.

Still sound in wind, limb, and stamina, they are finally forced to settle, not for the quality of golf they had always hoped to play, but for a pleasant weekly knock-around with friends. Dreams of a respectable handicap, which seemed so attainable at the start, missed by an unbelievable 15 strokes or more and never to come close to 90 in competitive play.

Few will give up completely. Bemused by the sheer volume of how-to fixes which, if they work at all, seem always to break down within a round or two, these 90-plus shooters will continue to search in vain for the definitive lesson, piece of literature, or film which really will cut a dozen strokes from their scores. Anything at all which might give them a clear and permanent understanding of the two-second process that is a correctly struck golf shot.

2

On Teaching

Generally speaking, teachers of golf are a lugubrious lot and with good reason. They compare rather well with the old prospectors for gold in that both are aware that they may labor a lifetime with scarcely a glimpse of pay dirt. Once in a while they may see the gleam of a small nugget, but sight of the mother lode is granted to very few.

Fortunately, the pessimism common to such professionals is usually accompanied by the wryest of humor. It's a combination that can be surprisingly companionable.

The difficulty they face, of course, is the fact that the subject they teach is over in the blinking of an eye. There is so little content in a two-second golf swing, but what there is, is profound and the permutation of words used in its description infinite.

Just why should an effective golf swing be so heartbreaking a thing to learn? And if many great people are to be believed, even more of a heartbreak to teach? The answer to that question is absence of clarity. Even the infinite permutation of description will often complicate and obscure the subject. This process can steadily sap the morale of both teacher and pupil.

Nevertheless, the teacher must continue to try spin upon spin in an attempt to clarify for the pupil what few teachers and even fewer great players ever succeed in making clear at all.

What would a teacher not give for an order of words to satisfactorily describe the paths *(note the plural)* that the clubhead must be made to take on its two-second journey from start-back to release—the moves that will put the clubhead on the first of these paths on the way up, and above all the moves that will put it on the second of these paths—*a different one, for they are not the same path*—on the way down.

An order of words as clear as crystal to be readily understood and acted upon by all save those seriously challenged by the imperviousness of their gray matter.

Any teacher able to impart an understanding that within a season will secure for beginners a handicap of, say, 18, then bring second and third season players down from 18 to 10 and to keep on doing it, is on the way to riches beyond his dreams. It can be done. In fact, it *has* been done by a few great men who learned from others "how to learn" and were then able to teach it to their pupils, and it put them on the road to golfing stardom.

Since the Second World War ended in 1945, increasing numbers of golf courses and practice ranges have made one-to-one instruction more readily available than ever before. The overall pattern of it has changed little, being a busy one in a passing trade of novice golfers booking half a dozen lessons at an early stage "just to get me started"—a number of follow-ups by some prepared to try again after an unsatisfactory year or two of hacking it round, and just a very few honing a game well into single figures. These latter already number among the top five percent of all who play golf and need not concern us here.

Millions more begin to play and continue to play for many years without resorting to lessons at all. One must conclude that any advancement they enjoy is dependent upon literary instruction from the bookstalls and/or the purchase or renting of videos that now form a considerable part of what might be termed "secondary" golf instruction, the demand for which seems quite insatiable.

Over the last 50 years book and magazine editors

have from time to time wondered whether or not satura-
tion in instruction had been reached. Just two or three
years ago a number of magazines reviewed their content
by use of subscriber survey in a creditable attempt to
look at the priorities from the customers' point of view.
The returns came in loud and clear: instruction, instruction, and more instruction was the first requirement of
the readership.

With the bargain in golf tuition always being between
willing sellers and exceedingly willing buyers, nothing
could be more natural than that the greatest teachers and
exponents of the game should need little persuading to
bring the secrets of their success to such an expanding
market.

No one can deny that it has been thoroughly well
done. What in most publications had been a pictorially
assisted lesson of perhaps three or four pages each month
quickly escalated to well-organized and balanced sec-
tions of 25 pages or more covering every facet of shot
making. There is absolutely no sign of this avalanche
abating.

The paradox is that excluding the occasional bizarre
nine-day-wonder method of teaching golf, which from
time to time will find space in golfing publications, vir-

tually all other orthodox instruction available is technically sound as far as it goes. Yet the amazing thing about it all seems an almost total absence of any kind of positive feedback from the subscribers.

If the proffered instruction has any measurable value it seems reasonable to expect a considerable number of ecstatic letters from grateful readers or viewers attesting to the help derived from a particular book, article, or video which had led to reductions in handicaps of 10 or a dozen strokes.

Surely not all beneficiaries of such a boon can be secretive scrooges. If a particular publication or video seriously advanced the games of a couple of thousand 90-shooters, one would think the dam of secrecy would burst and the attention drawn to it would begin to shrink the wide margin of skill between the pro and the duffer.

At the very heart of any learning process lies repetition, which will be used extensively in this book from now on. Perhaps this is as good a time as any to begin by repeating just what the margin is.

Remember that the world's golfers deserving of an expert rating, male and female, comprise just .00003 percent of all that play. Those with a handicap of nine or less account for a further 10 percent. All these have already earned the pleasure of consistent correct striking with its subsequent eradication of costly poor shots. Therefore, it is most unlikely that they will read anything of further value to them here.

Those who play between 10 and 18 constitute 30 percent of the total and may derive some benefit if they care to read on. The rest, close to sixty percent of all that play, are firmly stuck with handicaps between 19 and 45 or have no handicap at all, stuck because they have no idea of where the clubhead is or how it gets where it is as they swing it. Worse, they lack all knowledge of where the clubhead must be put on the way down or how to put it there.

The bulk of these high handicap players will hit 60 or more full shots in every round. They will hit 50,000 full shots every 10 years, and very few (if any) will be correctly struck. And it will be that way for as long as they play. Was there ever a more propitious area for dramatic improvement?

Any player of average strength and fitness—or not, for remember that the physically handicapped and even a few who were seriously ill have also succeeded at this game—who sees a reflection of his swing and his ignorance of the fundamentals in the blunt couple of paragraphs above, is but a step away from the road which can only lead to better things. If he is prepared to dismantle everything in order to improve, he must in the first instance take a hard look at the shortcomings in his knowledge of the basics of the game.

Most eminent writers on golf agree that the basics—once learned—will produce a reliable, powerful, and repeating swing. If he reads what the right people have put down on paper, the novice will find that these basics are generally simple and surprisingly few. He will find a choice of descriptions of these vital movements (which, of course, will vary from author to author), but each will boil down to ensuring that the clubhead arrives at the ball (1) on the correct path, (2) square to the line, and (3) at full speed. *In that order.*

As a guide, but only as a guide, it may be of help to suggest two or three great golfers turned author whose instruction books are considered to be among the very best in teaching the essentials of the swing.

Harvey Penick was a gentle, modest humanist revered by many as the greatest teacher the game has yet known.

Tommy Armour could hardly be more different. A Scotsman and an out-and out extrovert who won distinction in World War I, on the fairways as a champion golfer, and later on the lesson tees of Florida where he became the highest paid teaching pro of his time.

The third has already been introduced in the previous chapter: an amateur who achieved immortality on the golf course, winning 13 major titles in just eight years. His most notable accomplishment, of course, was the winning of the Open and Amateur Championships of both the United States of America and Great Britain in a single season: the "Impregnable Quadrilateral" of golf. With nothing further to prove, Bobby Jones retired from competitive play at the young age of 28. He laid no claim to great success as a teacher, but as early as 1930 had identified what to him was a quite unnecessary difference in skills within the game. His solutions really do give hope to any prepared to dismantle a feeble swing and to begin again from scratch.

Harvey Penick

Long before he died in 1997 at the ripe old age of 92, Harvey Penick was regarded as one of the best teachers of golf that America has yet produced—many would say the very best. A product of the caddie yard, Harvey eventually advanced as a golfer to the highest level. As a professional, he competed against the likes of Walter Hagen, Bobby Jones, Horton Smith, and Jimmy Demaret, all of whom (and many others) he came to know well and to study closely.

Later came Sam Snead, Byron Nelson, and Ben Hogan. In one of his books, Penick wrote that his vocation as a teacher and not as a touring professional was made clear to him the very first time he saw "Slammin'" Sam hit a golf ball.

As the longtime golf coach at the University of Texas in Austin, he did much to develop the golf scholarship system that resulted in American golf dominating all and sundry for more than 40 years. Penick was also the head professional at Austin Country Club for over 50 years. Upon his retirement in 1973 he became Emeritus Professional at Austin CC, but continued to advise the famous and the not so famous in his inimitable style right up to the time of his death.

For most of his life this quiet American was largely unknown outside of his own country. When Harvey was well into his 80s, however, this changed dramatically. The reason was because he was persuaded by writer Bud Shrake to publish the notes that he had compiled over a lifetime in golf that until then had been for his eyes only. How fortunate for all lovers of golf the publishing of his notes has proved to be.

His first two books received enormous appreciation the world over, many people admitting that once started, they read on from cover to cover at a single sitting. But beware. Therein lies danger.

Whimsical poems, anecdotes, reflections, and homilies come so thick and fast and each so charming that in the reading it becomes all too easy to lose sight of the golf instruction.

Enjoy Penick's books first time around. They are a marvelous read. Then start again, slowly and with a red pen with which to underline or box-in the elements that Harvey saw as essential to his teaching. Throughout his long career he wrote them down so that none of them would escape his memory when seeking to help a pupil.

Underline each piece of instruction or advice that strikes a chord with you, then read them again and again. It will not be difficult, because in the 350 pages that comprise both books you may use your pen surprisingly little. Nevertheless, each few words underlined will assist your understanding of the basics you simply must learn if you are ever to play to your full potential.

Could there ever be a more succinct or valuable summary of his work than can be found at the end of his *Little Green Golf Book* ? (published in the United States as *And If You Play Golf You Are My Friend*. Simon & Schuster 1993):

> Everything I say and do in my teaching is trying to produce these three things:
>> Path of the club.
>> Angle of the clubface.
>> Clubhead speed at impact.

Box-in Harvey's summary in double lines of red, for we shall see as we move on that he has listed the defining characteristics of all great players. These are, or should be, the basis of all good teaching. The sequence is of the greatest importance for without mastery of the first it is not possible to master the others. Master the first and apply it as the very essence of your swing. The remaining two—though of equal importance—will then become a surprisingly simple matter of fine-tuning.

Penick's work is recommended here as required reading for all high handicap golfers not because it is relatively new. In fact it is not new at all, much of it being jotted down in the 1930s and 1940s. No, Penick's greatest value to all wishing to learn the game comes through his pages in far subtler form.

The letters of appreciation from many of the world's great players speak volumes, but nowhere does this modest and thoughtful man claim credit for having run a production line of Hall of Fame golfers. Certainly there were many with whom he played a major part in shaping a highly successful career—Betsy Rawls, Tom Kite, Ben Crenshaw, and many others. Nowhere, however, does he seek credit for the successful careers of a host of already great players who called on him "for a little bit of help here and there."

Penick also finds space to describe other players of his tutelage or acquaintance of whom we have never heard. Players who for one reason or another had declined to go on to a championship career yet are lovingly remembered by him as among the greatest golfers he "had ever had the privilege to see."

Above all Penick never misses an opportunity to give full credit to what he called "self-made players." Babe Didrickson Zaharias and Byron Nelson are among those players listed who at the very start discovered exactly what they must learn and "how to learn it." Many self-made players have gone on to wonderful careers due almost entirely to their own intelligence and perspicacity.

In Great Britain we would call them "self-taught" players and we do have a few (LPGA member Laura Davies perhaps being the most successful). Self-taught players provide a permanent example that thoroughly learned principles and subsequent self-teaching is the key to further advancement. Learning "how to learn" will take a player down from 24 to 10, or from 36 to 18, just as surely as it helped Zaharias, Nelson, and Davies win great championships.

Tommy Armour

Tommy Armour was a contemporary of Harvey Penick, but more differing styles of writing on golf are impossible to imagine. Armour was a Scotsman whose Edinburgh University education saw him commissioned as an officer in World War I, during which he was seriously wounded. Following the war, in 1920, he immigrated to the United States.

While playing in America, Armour had a glittering career. His 24 victories included the 1927 U.S. Open and the 1930 PGA Championship. He also won the British

Open in 1931. When his career was over, Tommy became a highly respected teacher of golf, mainly in Florida.

As a youngster, Tommy took lessons to learn how to play golf. What he paid for those lessons he doesn't say in his famous book, only that somewhere he found the cash for lessons by the hundred, all of them in Great Britain. Glancing through the list of his many instructors one can believe that finding the cash to pay them could well have been a struggle.

From that list Armour singles out Harry Vardon, George Duncan, James Braid, J.H. Taylor, and the great J. Douglas Edgar as far and away the most gifted in that "they hammered in the simple foundations and taught me how to set about learning them." Those last few words are still the most profound that anyone will ever read in any book of golf instruction—or instruction on any other subject for that matter—telling us as they do of the other half of the contract between teacher and pupil or author and reader.

J. Douglas Edgar, incidentally, "a genius with a golf club" Bobby Jones once said of him, was later to produce and market his famous "Gate to Golf" device. The device consisted of a set of four small black rubber blocks complete with diagrams of how to place them into differing positions through which the clubhead simply had to pass if it was not to scatter them to the four winds.

The blocks could be placed to assist the clubhead onto any desired path on the hitting stroke. In to out, out to in, in to square to in, and also for the paths required for deliberate fades and draws.

Edgar, who hailed from Northumberland, was yet another Northerner who sought his fortune in North America where his successful playing and teaching career was to be cut short by his being murdered under mysterious circumstances.

Late in his career, Armour—like Penick—began to commit his thoughts on golf instruction to paper, leading to the publication of his very different *How to Play Your Best Golf All the Time* (Hodder & Stoughton 1954).

Armour's pithy writing is short, simple, and direct in the extreme. Straight from the shoulder he tells his pupils that a good golf game can "never be bought by the page, the pound, or by the hour—or even bought."

He taught simplicity and economy of time and effort by profitable concentration on similar essentials to those so clearly summarized by Penick. When following his advice Armour called upon his pupils to use their brains and to practice what he taught as the indispensable elements of good golf. Any pupil not prepared to learn "how to learn" had his lessons summarily called off. All this from a teacher who as far back as 1940 was charging 100 dollars an hour and who never seemed to be without a pupil on the practice tee.

Armour put his finger on it when he wrote that, "Six people wish to be taught golf to every one that truly wishes to learn." Those six, of course, are included in the mass of players who only figure in competitive golf after deducting a handicap of 20 or more.

He resented criticism of professional teachers who he saw as being generally most competent. He would react quickly, pinpointing serious shortcomings in pupils—lazy-mindedness in many which rendered them unable to profit fully from any lesson. It irked him to see both men and women "who might have been good players had they but knuckled down to master the one simple element of good golf—the paths of the clubhead—instead of losing their way by wandering in a maze of detail."

Armour concentrated on what he saw as the eternal truths of the game, doing all he could to teach his pupils how to learn them. When that was completed he would encourage them to advance by their own determination and hard work.

To assist the readers of his book Armour highlighted salient points in bold, red type. Once again there are startlingly few of them, a reminder of a famous remark by Walter Hagen. On being asked to consider writing about golf, Hagen replied, "I don't believe I will, as all I know about golf could easily be written on a postcard." (The truth of which will be demonstrated later.)

As correct as Armour's teaching undoubtedly was, experience had taught him to not expect too much from his pupils. This is clearly expressed in the dedication that he wrote for his book.

> With my esteem and gratitude this book is dedicated to the ever-aspiring golfers.
> The Lord must love them; He made so many of them.

This monumental piece of cheek, however, appeared to have little or no effect upon the demand for his book or for his services on the practice tee.

Teachers of golf are a lugubrious lot are they not? But with the wryest sense of humor.

Bobby Jones

Robert Tyre Jones Jr. did not consider himself a teacher of the game in any formal sense. An amateur throughout his short but incredibly successful career, he undoubtedly benefited from advice he received from Stewart Maiden. Maiden was yet another émigré Scot and the professional at Jones's home club at East Lake Country Club in Atlanta, Georgia.

Stewart was of the old school of Scottish golf teachers and was considered by Penick to be the best in the business. He was also in the same mold as the men retained by Armour for knowing precisely what must be learned and for being able to tell a pupil how to learn it. Maiden's influence on both Penick and Jones must have been considerable.

Considering his outstanding competitive career it's somewhat surprising that Jones played a relatively small amount of recreational golf. He regularly declined games in the summer because it was "too hot," and he seldom touched his clubs in the winter because it was "much too cold." During his "golden years" of the 1920s he was also in the process of earning two degrees: Mechanical Engineering from Georgia Tech and English Literature from Harvard. Afterward, he began studying the law at Emory University and was able to pass the state bar examination when just halfway into his second year of school. Prior to entering any major championship, however, Jones did practice very hard indeed. And it paid off; he won an astonishing 62 percent of all that he entered.

To read anything Jones wrote is to share in his great intellect and power of observation. At the time of his remarks on the disproportionate ratio of skills within the game, it was his opinion that most average players were lacking any knowledge as to where the clubhead must be, how to put it there, or how to keep it there.

In his observations of thousands of average players swinging a golf club to the top, however, he could find little fault. "Most players advance this far with fair success," he wrote, "but it is the next step that usually trips them."

Jones was at a complete loss to understand why so many millions of people, obviously in love with the game, could be so wildly out of touch with the few essentials of the correct stroke when the remedy was plain. When faced with scores continually in the high 90s, it seemed to him ridiculous that a golfer should carry on pigheadedly, making no attempt to learn the one or two essential elements that would immediately improve matters.

He did not believe in luck or kindly providence. He believed in cause and effect. He saw the cause of almost all poor shots as failure to set and hold the clubhead on its correct path in the hitting stroke. The remedy he saw was simple self-education.

These three authors are offered for their simplicity and common objective. That they are all pleasurable to read is an added bonus. Yes, they are from a past generation. But before dismissing them as old hat, remember that it is questionable if more recent books have done as much for the novice of today as theirs did for the budding player 80 years ago.

There are of course very many more. Recent ones have the advantage of being more readily obtained, but at an early stage the proliferation of diagrams and photographs can add complexity and unwanted complication for the novice or swing rebuilder.

In the first instance they would do well to acquire a full understanding of the paths of the clubhead and make that their prime concern.

3

On Learning

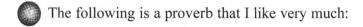 The following is a proverb that I like very much:

When you first come to know that you do not know, you come to know a very great deal.

Probably first expressed by an erudite man at the lifting of some great fog of ignorance, he could have handed no finer focus to the average golfer determined to inquire exactly what it is that he does not know about the golf swing.

There are 25 million average golfers. If just half of them would accept that they do not know enough about the swing, and decide to find out—through what follows here and/or other means—then the narrowing of the margins of skill could be considerable.

To tell the owner of a flawed golf swing that if he wants to strike the ball correctly he must first acquire an understanding of the shape of the thing he is trying to produce, would seem to be sound advice. However, the tutor or author should not complain if he is then asked to describe the particular shape he has in mind.

The answer is usually given in the form of a demonstration swing by the pro or a four-shot photo sequence in the book, neither of which advances anything. Descriptions of each facet of the swing immediately follow, but after the lesson, still with no clear picture to work on the lonely practice knock can be heartbreaking.

Nor does a demo swing give the student much idea of the major differences between the two paths that the clubhead must be made to follow. In the absence of coordinates, Pythagoras himself would have difficulty determining where the clubhead must be and how to keep it there.

There can be no doubt that a thorough understanding of the two paths is essential to the successful playing of any full golf shot. In defining the position of a clubhead at any point on either of these paths, the use of the word "laterally" takes on major importance. No other single word is perfect for the job and it is vital that its exact meaning is clearly understood:

If a player stands erect, arms outstretched from the sides with palms facing to the front, any object to the front of his palms, be it an inch or a mile away or at any level from the ground upwards, can be said to be laterally to the front of him. Similarly, any object to the rear of his knuckles can be said to be laterally to the rear of him.

Almost everyone who plays golf has a reasonable idea of the shape of the backswing, which takes the clubhead on a path from the ball to its position at the top. It is a relatively languid movement, carrying the clubhead to its fullest extension at the waist before it disappears as it gets to be laterally behind the player around the level of his right shoulder. Then up and round it goes to the position at the top from which it will change direction.

The hitting stroke then returns the clubhead along an entirely different path. Down and round from behind the player to reappear as it gets to be laterally to the front at about the level of his right knee, arriving at the ball on a shallow angle and from inside the ball-to-target line.

For any shot to be struck correctly, the makeup of these differing paths must be thoroughly learned. Give or take a percentage point or two, what must be learned is this:

When the clubhead is swung from the ball to the top, 60 percent of the total length of that path is laterally to the front of the player. The other 40 percent is laterally to the rear of the player.

When the clubhead returns from the top to the ball,

however, 70 percent of the total length of that path is laterally to the rear of the player. The other 30 percent is laterally to the front of the player.

Put another way, the clubhead is behind the player for just 40 percent of the length of his backswing, but must be held behind him for 70 percent of the length of his hitting stroke.

> The average golfer's problem is not so much a lack of ability as it is a lack of knowing exactly what it is that he must do.
>
> —Ben Hogan, 1957

What comes next is a somewhat less exciting, but absolutely necessary examination of the facets of the swing that make it possible for a player to hold his clubhead laterally behind him for over two-thirds of the distance it must travel to the ball.

For the clubhead to be held to the rear for a much longer distance coming down than was the case going up, the plane of its downswing path must be made to change, but with no change at all in its vertical axis. This is one of the most important "buts" in golf.

A transference of some of the player's weight to his

left foot and leg both changes the plane *and* supplies the only power required to pull the top assembly into position just above the waist. This position is one that Ben Hogan believed to be crucial to the success of every full shot. (Fully described at the end of chapter eight, this is the only position from which a correct release of the clubhead can be made.)

Not one moment before the transfer of weight has both powered and lowered an unchanged top assembly to its correct position above the right hip, do the arms or hands turn on any power of their own.

Once a golfer has grasped "exactly what it is that he must do," he is bound to compare it with what it was that he had previously been doing, often for many years.

It will not be lost on him that the discrepancy between the clubhead returning correctly to the front at the level of his right knee, and the clubhead returning incorrectly to the front at the level of his neck (or higher) has been as much as three or four feet!

I do not understand why so many people can be so wildly out of touch with the essentials of the correct stroke.

—Bobby Jones ca. 1930

Was there ever a more courteous way of pointing out to three-quarters of all who play the game that their clubhead is three feet off track on each full shot they ever make?

Just about as "wildly out of touch" as it is possible to be.

When swinging with a built-in error of that magnitude, how can any player hope to strike the ball effectively?

When questioning average golfers on their knowledge of the swing, most knew that the clubhead should disappear behind him or her at about the level of the right shoulder as it can be plainly seen to do. However, on the downswing (hitting stroke), the consensus was that it reappears to the front somewhere between the level of the waist and the neck. A few went for the head and one or two for 12 inches higher than that. Few, if any, were aware that the clubhead must somehow be made to get to the front at the level of the right knee. So where in the name of heaven does the thing go so badly wrong?

The thing goes wrong in that most instruction covers the *plane* of the swing just as it covers the *path* of the clubhead. Seldom, if ever, does it extend to *planes* and *paths* plural. Too many would-be golfers leave the practice tee with the belief that there is one plane and one path.

That the downswing "mirrors the backswing" is a classic piece of sophistry still often taught today. The downswing must do no such thing.

The downswing plane, in fact, must be made to change. If it doesn't, the position of the clubhead as it gets to the front can never be on track. When path and plane are being taught and the sole example is the backswing, it must be made clear that there is a second, quite different, plane for the downswing that sets the clubhead on a second, quite different path. It is this change to a second plane and path that leads the clubhead correctly to the front at the level of the knee, so well described and illustrated in Hogan's *Five Lessons*.

Until that is crystal clear, the teaching of the plane of the swing cannot be synonymous with the teaching of the position of the clubhead. If a pupil is ever to learn exactly what it is that he is trying to do, the position of the clubhead coming down must take precedence over the plane of the swing going up.

The purpose of these early chapters has been to bring to the attention of high and middle handicappers that their present lowly position in the scheme of things is far and away the one with the greatest potential for improvement. In other words, they have nowhere to go but forward. The lower the handicap the more difficult becomes the squeezing out of each further shot as one attempts to lower it still further. The higher the handicap then far greater is the possibility of a dramatic reduction.

When one sees thousands more bad golfers than good ones, bluntness in addressing the bad ones becomes excusable and necessary. The idea is not to add to despondency but to lift it, to assure all who have given up hope of ever acquiring a better game that the possibility does exist. What is required is that the essentials of which they have little or no understanding be made crystal clear to them.

Desire for advancement boils down to two things: The first is to know with certainty what it was that they did not know; the second is their own determination to learn it and to reap great benefit from it.

The concept of teaching oneself "how to learn" is in no way exclusive to golf; it applies equally to any skill, art, or craft. The mastery of it, however, depends upon the understanding and absolute acceptance of one or several axiomatic truths which govern success or failure within that craft.

Master craftsmen come in both genders. Within sense and reason, depending upon the craft concerned, they may be of any age—young and athletic or old and perhaps somewhat decrepit, but all become masters of it. Each able to produce a thing of beauty at which others, ignorant of their inner knowledge and discipline in learning, can only marvel. Golf is just such a craft.

Talent? God-given gift? It is nothing of the sort. Their mastery has come from a proper induction into the fundamentals recognized as essential to their skill. A careful study and subsequent understanding of those fundamentals followed by enlightenment. They have discovered "how to learn." From there on in—other than for the very finest of tuning—further advancement comes through their thought and effort.

He is the brave man who is prepared to offer a reason for the sad lot of today's average golfer. In large part the reason lies in the history of the expansion of the game. Yet Bobby Jones's puzzlement that so many should fail to recognize their ignorance of what he saw as just a few essentials and to apply them to their swings is perfectly understandable.

Jones believed that destructive preconceptions acquired by playing with no knowledge of those essentials was the cause of most, if not all, poor swings. The remedy, he believed, lay in insisting that all novices seeking lessons should first have a broad formal induction to the game in order that they receive a thoroughly accurate conception of what goes into the making of a proper stroke before progressing to actual play.

Such preteaching as seen in college golf in America is why that system has enjoyed and continues to enjoy so much success in the production of expert golfers. Elsewhere in the world however, preteaching has been at best a piecemeal business—a complete nonstarter in British golf until comparatively recently. And it's an omission for which British golf continues to pay a heavy price today.

We are left with the question of why the average golfer appears to draw so little measurable benefit from the volume of instruction that is readily available to him. In fairness to the player, the possibility that he has read widely in an attempt to improve should not be discounted. But with secondary instruction it is all too easy to become bemused and discouraged by what seems to many a complex and unmanageable mass of information. Simplicity and clarity is what is looked for, but these two are seldom found together.

It is for this reason that both primary and secondary instruction has earlier been described as being sound "only as far as it goes." In many cases both could and should go further by recognizing that much is at best vague and incomplete, as well as by anticipating what might reasonably be foreseen as unanswered questions in the mind of the novice.

In a previous chapter, repetition was mentioned as being at the very heart of teaching and learning. Its importance to a student of golf, or of any other serious subject, cannot be overemphasized. How many, in the study of a subject they desperately wish to learn, can assimilate all in a single reading of a textbook? So, with all principal facts which you would have firmly planted into your psyche, read, read again, and then reread in order that they will be present in the mind at the vital moment that determines the success or failure of every shot.

Let us consider Harvey Penick's words on the importance of repetition. In compiling his "Teachers' Guide" that he began in 1929, he wrote:

[In] golf instruction the principles are easy to learn, but useless unless they are put into action. [In] golf instruction the principles are also easy to forget. I need to read them every few days.

If it was good enough for Harvey Penick it should be good enough for us.

There is much repetition of principles in the following chapters, but there is no apology for it. It is never too late to dismantle and rebuild an ineffective swing. If you recognize yours as such, then decide at once to scrap it. Start today! You have already missed the first buttonhole. Unless you are awake to it, you will never button-up.

4

"Such a Little Secret"

secret: The key to a mystery, the governing principle
of anything, known only to the initiated.
—*Modern University Dictionary*

When switching on the television to watch a golf
championship, few expect to see or hear something
that will change their whole concept of the golf swing
and set them on the road to a greatly improved game.
The realization is that there really is a master key to good
golf.

The realization that a player with good knowledge
of the fundamentals of the swing will never make them
function correctly if he is without that master key. Para-
doxically, that a player ignorant of the fundamentals, but
aware of the master key, can quickly come to play good
golf by a thorough learning and application of the
few essentials of which he had been previously unaware.
With one proviso—that the master key be paramount
throughout.

It is of little consequence where, when, and who the player was. Fickle memory says Birkdale in 1976, Johnny Miller on his record roll. The precise details are no longer clear, but following the umpteenth superb drive by the player, a 30-second aside between two friends is perfectly well remembered.

As usual, BBC Television was being served by those most stylish of golf conversationalists Peter Alliss and Henry Longhurst. Alliss remarked: "There goes another, right down the middle. My word Henry, he certainly has the secret today."

"Yes he has," Longhurst replied, "and you know Peter, it is such a little secret. He is swinging so beautifully that as one watches one immediately notices the fact that his right ear is held absolutely still until the ball is struck. Motionless until impact, it then moves in a surprising direction. To his right, away from the target. If, as we swing, we pay much more attention to the parts which do not move at all, or move only very little, might we not better control the parts that do?"

For all who dream of coming to grips with rebuilding their swings, the nub of the thing is this: From the moment of start-back until the clubhead strikes the ball, the right ear must remain firmly in position.

Everyone who ever played golf should know of the

importance of swinging the club beneath a still head. It is the very first essential mentioned by a tutor or any elementary book of golf instruction. Unfortunately it is no longer hammered home as once it was. Too often now a mention is all it gets and the pupil is the loser.

This confusing change of emphasis on a vital part of the swing came about a few years ago. The idea was that it was better to permit *some* movement of the head, rather than have the player feel inhibited by the notion that the head must be fixed vicelike throughout the stroke.

While there is reasoning behind the argument that the head should be permitted some movement as the stroke is made, in the mind of a novice this can come to mean that a steady head is not essential. Therefore, he no longer sees it as the overriding principle that governs his effort to swing the clubhead along the correct paths on both the backswing and hitting stroke.

Unless immediately rectified, this misconception can permanently undermine his every attempt at improvement. Far better that permissible movement of the head had not been mentioned at all.

This apparent contradiction is of such importance to the golfer that it ought not to be passed over in a couple of short paragraphs. The very object of this book is to exhort the high handicap player to abandon a swing that has never produced satisfactory results, by putting his absolute belief in rebuilding it around a motionless right ear.

Until the new swing is thoroughly ingrained he must not be sidetracked by misunderstood theories on movement of the head that can so easily negate the success of his swing rebuild.

For those players sidetracked long ago, high handicappers who have played for some considerable time with no improvement, the confusion probably arose with a misleading question. Should the head move or should it not? This was no doubt followed by an incorrect assumption that it cannot do both.

Thereafter the head is permitted to move, usually destructively leftward with the swing, as may be seen on golf courses almost anywhere one cares to look. The short answer is that it *can* do both. The right ear can remain quite still while the left ear and left side of the face can move reasonably freely.

If a point on the surface of a sphere is fixed in its position, it does not follow that all other points on the sphere are similarly fixed. Far from it. With virtually no movement at the fixed point, slight movement may occur around it that steadily increases until the greatest movement available is to be seen at a point farthest from that which is fixed.

In the case of a golfer's head, this is the movement that is deemed permissible—some would say *desirable*. Slight movement of the left side of the face and the left ear is discernible in the swings of most great players. The right ear, however, is held quite motionless until impact.

If he thinks of it at all, the movement deemed permissible by the average player almost always involves the whole of the head. It is present to some extent in every swing he makes. Even half swings and little hands and arms shots.

A destructive movement of the head, which occurs with the high handicap golfer on virtually every shot, is usually forced upon the player by some other fault in his swing. Forced means forced. He is unable to help himself. Careless involuntary movement of the head above an otherwise sound swing is comparatively rare.

For whatever reason the head has moved, having done so it then becomes impossible for the player to strike the ball correctly.

The damage done depends upon the direction and distance over which the head has been forced to move.

Poorly struck shots are produced by all players with swings that allow the head to move forward. That is to say *leftward* with the stroke, which milks it of all power. The head may also be forced upward, a less repetitive condition, but every bit as destructive. On occasion the head may be *jerked* rather than moved, both leftward and upward simultaneously, again caused by serious faults or omissions elsewhere in the swing. This is absolutely guaranteed to produce the total collapse of the stroke so embarrassing to the onlooker.

Henry Longhurst observed that Johnny Miller's right ear moved backward, away from the target as the ball was struck. Harvey Penick tells us that Byron Nelson's head could similarly be seen to move backward at impact, often by several inches. Both are perfect examples of Newton's Law of Motion: For every action there is an equal and contrary reaction.

Such a contrary reaction is seen only in the expert player who can swing the clubhead along its correct lower path in the hitting stroke—delivering it at maximum speed and with the clubface angled exactly as required by the shot to be made.

A contrary reaction is never seen in the average golfer whose ineffective swing delivers none of these things.

In his aside to Alliss, all of Longhurst's emphasis

was on the motionless right ear. It is significant that he never once mentioned the head. Let us distill his remark still further and concentrate upon an even smaller point: the right aural canal, or in plain English, the right ear hole.

In any focus of concentration, the smaller the focal point the greater is one's sensitivity to it. To continue to use the word ear would do, and in a television broadcast it was probably a more genteel choice than use of the vernacular. Distilling the focal point down to the quarter inch diameter of the aural canal, however, will give a golfer a far sharper image in the mind than the more vague outline of the whole of the right ear.

If all golfers had perforated eardrums then to focus on the perforation would give the sharpest possible image of that which he must hold quite still. As they do not, the right ear hole is the best available to us. The word will be used as little as possible, but remains the image that the golfer should concentrate upon at any subsequent mention of the right ear.

Interestingly, if concentration upon the right ear hole gives us a sharper image than concentration upon the whole ear, then how much less sharp must be the image when the golfer is asked to concentrate upon the whole of the head? This may well be the reason why teachers of golf have had so little success in fixing its importance in the minds of their pupils.

In dismantling an ineffective swing and rebuilding anew, the right ear hole is quite definitely the point at which all high handicappers should start.

Determine today that henceforth every stroke you play will be made under, around, and above a perfectly still right ear hole. Make it your rebuild resolution and never break it.

If all of this has struck a chord with you, by now you have already left your chair to make a swing—no club necessary—under a fixed right ear hole. You will have found it surprisingly simple and it may have given you focus. The missing anchor, perhaps, at the top of the gyro. A top anchor of great assistance to those at the bottom, your feet.

With so many millions of 90-plus golfers out there, there may be thousands who will find this easily forgotten principle to be their only missing link. They may be well acquainted with the paths along which the clubhead simply must be swung, and aware of the small adjustments needed to bring the clubface square to the ball. The head, however, has been moving imperceptibly leftward with each stroke, dragging the right ear with it. Forced to turn down the wick to limit the damage, they

Make every stroke you play under,
around, and above a still right ear.

no longer achieve maximum speed. The price has been a frustrating loss of all the old power in their shots.

If this chapter has restored to memory a long-forgotten element in their swings, enabling them to once again apply maximum speed at the ball, then all the luck in the world to them. The only resolution they will need to make is never again to forget such a little secret.

There remain the millions who need to rebuild from scratch. Within its membership every golf club in the world holds a percentage of them. Usually about 75 percent. Likeable, stoical, and whimsical would sum up most of these players. If perpetual high scoring produces a morose and cranky golfer, he quickly finds himself without a partner and eventually quits the game.

Most high handicappers play on for many years enjoying their inconsequential social rounds of course, but seldom breaking 95 from the competition tees. Unaware of the upper anchor of the gyro that the fixed right ear hole provides, they have missed the first buttonhole. Despite endless remedies, each with a life span of just a few holes, very few ever manage to button up correctly.

Determine to rebuild just once more. You are now initiated in the governing principle of the correctly struck golf shot. You have the master key. Believe in it absolutely. It is the key you require to unlock the mystery of

the wide margin of skill between yourself and better players of your acquaintance. There are other lesser keys to
be sure. But with this master key—the still right ear hole
firmly in place until the ball is struck—the other three or
four keys will come more easily to you.

Those still unconvinced have only to replay tapes of
Open or World Match Play Championships. Find a sequence of Ernie Els on a tee captured by a camera from
behind, looking down the ball-to-target line. Not because
he is Ernie Els—although that is bound to rivet the attention—but because he is a big man who will fill the screen
to prove a point.

Find the patience to work through his complete swing
with the "still/advance" mechanism. You will see a right
ear fairly skewered into position until the ball is struck.
Not until the ball starts on its way is there any discernible movement of it.

However many players' swings you observe in this
manner, the steady right ear hole will be common to all.
With tour players you will note that every practice swing
is given equally serious attention. From full practice
swings, little touch shots, to practice putts. Even with a
seemingly casual wave of the club while the shot is pon-
dered, the right ear hole can be seen to be held absolutely stationary.

Longhurst's little secret is worth its weight in eagles to the aspiring golfer, but simply swinging a club beneath a still right ear will not of itself produce a quality golf shot. Consistent correct striking requires that two or three fundamentals of the swing are thoroughly learned and applied under and around that still ear hole. We will be looking at these fundamentals soon.

Before moving on there is a further thing that can so easily be overlooked. It is never to forget that the positioning of the right ear when setting up—at address—remains entirely a matter for the player.

By that is meant that the player should always be aware of the amount of adjustment available to him as he settles to address. As the swing rebuild progresses and the now thoroughly learned basics fit into place, a great deal more benefit may be had from a finely tuned positioning of the right ear just before start-back.

All of this should come early on. It should give the player any amount of fun to experiment in adjusting the position to that which will extract the very maximum from his new swing. Once settled upon, it should be the position used for all shots played from a normal stance. Wherever the ear is finally placed, from start-back it must remain quite still until the ball is struck. High handicap players rarely consider that the position of the head—

which they now know as the right ear hole—is adjustable at all, almost all setting up with the ball opposite the left cheekbone for every shot they play.

If then on the hitting stroke there is a sway even further leftward, one sees the all too common sight of a player vainly trying to hit a ball that is virtually behind him.

In his instructional articles, Greg Norman advises that for long shots, the player should set up with the ball opposite the left armpit. This should be good enough for all

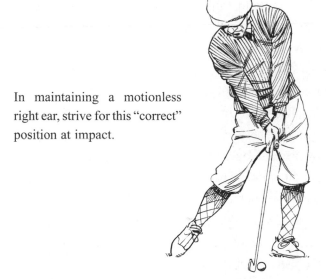

In maintaining a motionless right ear, strive for this "correct" position at impact.

of us. In most people the left ear is laterally three or four inches to the right of the left armpit. Therefore, at address, the left ear must be three or four inches to the right of the ball, thus fixing the lateral position of the right ear hole. Here the right ear hole must remain until the ball is on its way. This is what experts such as Greg Norman call "getting behind it and staying behind it," which the average golfer miserably fails to do on almost every shot.

The point is that as the new swing continues to develop, do not neglect to check that the position of the ear at address is that which gives the greatest feel of "rightness" to the stroke. This ability to make fine adjustments at address is valuable and each individual should make the very most of it until he finds the exact position which best fits his own particular swing.

We now have the rock solid foundations that Henry Longhurst's little secret gives. We must expunge from the mind all confusing arguments of permissible head movement and the fact that in the case of the expert the head may be seen to move to the player's right at impact.

These phenomena need not concern a golfer rebuilding his swing in a determined attempt to reduce his handicap from say 24 to 14 within two seasons.

You may now have a better understanding of the paths of the clubhead. You have coordinates (references) by the dozen that govern your stationary preliminaries and with luck the path of your backswing, which has never given much trouble. However, with the correct locus of the downswing so recently determined in your mind, as yet you can have none at all with which to govern it.

You probably know little of the invisible lines in golf which, if all else fails, can be a handy aid to keeping everything on the golfer's side of the ball as he does the best he can with an imperfect swing. You have doubtless heard of hitting from the top, schlaffing, spinning out, casting, and faulty timing together with a host of other indeterminate words and phrases, but can you define and eradicate them?

Do you transfer your weight correctly? Was there ever a more misleading term when what is meant is the transferring of *some* of your weight?

If your answer to all of this is an honest "no," then what we now know is that you do not know. Take heart! Remember the proverb: "When you first come to know that you do not know, you come to know a very great deal."

We can now move on to look more closely at the four elements that govern the correct stroke.

5

Rogue Elements

To remain a high handicapper for many years—having failed to grasp the significance of a couple of elementary moves within the swing—is very hard to take. The fact that 75 out of 100 fail as well is but small consolation.

One reason these moves go unlearned by so many is that they take place in the space of five one-hundredths of a second, which puts them almost within the subconscious. The movements are small and simple enough. Their description is anything but. It is little wonder that the great bulk of players seem doomed to struggle on with insufficient knowledge of them.

For a golf club to be swung to the greatest advantage, four elements must be present:

1. A steady head. (right ear hole)
2. Knowledge of the two paths along which the clubhead must be swung.

3. The shifting of some of the weight to the left foot and leg.
4. The correct first movement of the hands as the swing changes direction.

To ensure a steady head, at address the right ear must be set into a position best placed to ensure that the clubhead follows the correct paths and is allowed to drift nowhere else. Once set, the ear remains quite stationary, positioning the head well behind the ball, supplying a top anchor to the gyro and maintaining the radius of first the backswing and then the downswing until the ball is struck.

The second element is mental, not physical. It is simply to know with absolute certainty what it is that the player is about to do. He is about to set the clubhead along a constant path to the top of the swing, then bring it down along a constant path which will deliver it through the ball. (Important: These are not the same path.) As the clubhead is swung to the top—which most golfers can do with little difficulty—a correct plane, extension, and pivot will take it back, up, and round to get it to the rear of the player at about the height of his right shoulder.

On the hitting stroke, a correct weight-transfer will tilt the plane a little to the right of the target. The bent right elbow and wrists will guide the clubhead down and round from behind until it returns laterally to the front of the player at about the height of his right knee or even a shade lower.

Taken together these differing paths of the clubhead form the primary objective in any correctly played golf stroke. It's a relatively easy objective for those who are aware of these paths, but impossible for those who are not.

It is in the understanding of elements three and four that the handicap of the average golfer parts company with that of the better player. These two rogues—the transfer of some of the weight and the first movement of the hands as the clubhead starts down —are the fundamentals of the golf swing that separate the tiger from the rabbit, as it were. Fully learned and correctly applied by the better player, in a microsecond his clubhead is placed on the correct lower path of the hitting stroke. More often than not, the result is a well-struck shot.

Unlearned and consequently misapplied by the average player, the clubhead is never placed on the correct path down and through the ball. It arrives too quickly to the front of him—often at a point higher than his shoulder rather than at the level of his right knee. This is casting and nothing can now prevent a cut across the ball.

Any effectiveness remaining in the stroke is now dependent upon clubface alignment. Was it shut or open at impact? Was misalignment slight or severe? Effectiveness will also depend upon how much or how little he has been able to control the cut by spurious contortions made in lieu of the correct weight-transfer and correct start-down.

It is a curious thought that millions of players, having sacrificed these two small essentials, will spend years attempting to improve a fatally flawed swing when a few weeks of concentrated learning of the two missing movements would have set them up to play good golf.

Remember that Armour recognized this golfing condition 50 years ago and described it perfectly: "These men and women might have been good players had they but knuckled down to master the one simple element of good golf, the paths of the clubhead, instead of losing their way in a maze of detail of their own making."

The only exit from this maze lies in placing the clubhead on its correct paths by learning and applying the two principal moves that will put it there. There is no other way out.

Just why, in so many cases, the traditional pattern of teaching completely misses this mark is really quite extraordinary. The teaching has always been done in a strict sequence of the 10 or 12 items from grip to follow-through, which seems logical. Yet the fact remains that any novice who, at a very early stage, fails to transfer some of his weight and to guide his hands down correctly has little or no chance of ever breaking 90.

Failure here, more than any other reason, has condemned millions to a life of golf in the wilderness when things might have been so very different.

Grip, ball position, stance, posture, etc., must all be learned, of course. Most long handicappers who have played for years freely admit that shifting their weight has always been a mystery to them. Similarly, their knowledge of the correct first move down is virtually nonexistent.

Either primary and secondary instruction has failed in its description of what should happen at the top, or the players have failed to learn it. Revision and a re-sit are required. This time the player has much to help him that was absent at his first examination on this awkward subject.

Rogue elements three and four, weight transfer and first move down of the hands, are no longer free to balk a player's every attempt at progress. Yes, they do remain tricky. But now they are isolated by the top anchor of the gyro, which is present in every swing the player makes—even little swings and practice swings.

No matter what occurs in the first stages of learning this pair of movements, the player must trust the stationary right ear absolutely. He will at once enjoy the benefit of a constant radius in every stroke even if the rogues are not yet fully learned or correctly applied. The swing path down and through may not be quite correct, but the consistency in his swing will in its turn produce a constant pattern of shots, even though they may still be somewhat misdirected.

As transferring some of the weight and the start down of the hands improves with learning and practice, so the swing path down and through the ball will become more nearly correct.

Improvement of one's golf swing is yet to be found in Armour's "maze of detail" (nor on the road to Damascus). It only comes with knowledge of the correct and the incorrect: by building on what is known to be correct and by steadily eliminating what is known to be incorrect.

The little secret is the master key. The constant radius it supplies will, for the first time, render any adjustment the player decides is necessary both meaningful and measurable. As and when he becomes sufficiently confident to make these adjustments and assess their effect, he will realize that he knows "how to learn." He will have commenced to teach himself, and his rebuild will be well under way.

It should always be remembered that it is possible to execute weight transfer and start down perfectly, but in concert with undesirable head movement. When the head moves, be it ever so slightly, the radius must move with it, forcing the swing path to drift off track. Within the swing there is little that can be done to counteract a sway.

If old swaying habits return, movement of the right ear during the swing is the first thing to be looked for.

The swing paths, the weight transfer, and the first movement of the hands at the top are integral. Before going on to look at them in more detail, there are further factors of great assistance to anyone attempting to make these intractable moves of golf correctly: knowledge of coordinates and an understanding of the invisible lines.

6

Coordinates and the Invisible Lines

Before he begins to swing a club and make a shot, there are any number of things that must have the golfer's full attention. Pity the poor beginner then, so absorbed in these preliminaries that the bit that really matters seems impossible to accomplish without all that has gone before breaking down.

In consequence, little of his instruction on the all-important swinging and releasing of the clubhead remains with him. Uncertain of precisely what he is to do, the swing he does make is a puny thing. All thinking spent, through a fog of confusion one thing at least seems clear, that his next swing must be given more force. In his fashion he applies it by bringing a heave of the body to bear on the stroke.

Whether all of him sways to the front and to the left, or he turns semicorrectly, but without any transfer of his lower half, the stroke is ruined. Greater or lesser hoicks such as this are the commonest sight in golf. Either move will pull his right shoulder forward, throwing his hands to the front and the clubhead onto an out-to-in path, whence nothing can prevent it from cutting across the ball. He has hit helplessly from the top, as all inferior players seem bound to do.

At this vital early stage of shot preparation, the two rogue elements (the shifting of some of the weight to the left foot and leg and the correct first movement of the hands as the swing changes direction) are missed by millions and never learned thereafter. Whether it be lack of clarity or emphasis by the teacher, or insufficient attention by the pupil, rectification seldom happens. Between lessons the player begins to ingrain his casting of the clubhead. He may have some modest success with improvised adjustments designed to lessen the cut and improve alignment, but his place among the high handicappers is now assured. With a permanent out-to-in swing, any attempt to produce power in that way is made impossible, serving only to exaggerate the fault in every shot.

He will have seen and come to envy the position of the forearms of the better players at full release of the club, but with his now permanent out-to-in swing, any attempt to produce power in that way is made impossible, serving only to exaggerate the fault in every shot.

Neither is there a full follow-through. A classic finish is rarely seen at the completion of a faulty swing.

Should a player who casts the clubhead like a fly fisherman ever attempt a powerful release and classic finish, his right foot simply must lurch toward the target or he will fall heavily onto his right shoulder. All caused, said Bobby Jones, by sacrificing knowledge in favor of swinging incorrectly too soon and too often.

Glance sometime at the body language as pro and pupil trudge back from the practice tee. Those slumped shoulders and lowered heads are invariably due to the general failure of most golfers to grasp what must be done as the swing changes direction. A tripwire this, and the major cause of most golfing despair.

In his book *Bobby Jones on Golf,* Jones was completely at one with Armour when he wrote: "There are numberless players who devote enough thought, time and hard practice to the game to make them very good golfers if only they might start out with an accurate conception of what it is they want to do, but in so many instances there is confusion of ideas, making intelligent progress impossible."

The accurate conception that Jones urged all golfers to acquire was simply a thorough knowledge of the lo-

cus (path) that the clubhead must be made to follow in
the hitting stroke, and the use of personal coordinates to
reproduce that locus, shot upon shot.

Coordinates

Two or more factors used to define the exact position
of a geometrical line or plane which, when used
in order, produce a constant result.
Ancient Greek Geometrical Mathematics. ca. 500 B.C.

Ancient definition or not, it almost seems to have been
written to help golfers realize that with knowledge of the
correct locus to the ball, and the common sense to fix his
own coordinates, he at last knows "how to learn," and
that further advancement is possible.

Average golfers remain average golfers because what
coordinates they have cover only the stationary preliminaries, all used up before the swing has reached halfway.
There they run dry, knowing nothing of the two vital elements that simply must be learned by any player if he is
to set his clubhead on a correct powerful locus through
the ball.

Most golfers will play a lifetime without considering the value of coordinates at all. They have them of

A simple figure showing the basic (upright) path for the clubhead on the backswing and the shallow path taken on the downswing.

course, but the positioning of the hands on the grip, the alignment of the feet, hips, and shoulders, hands at address, position of the ball, etc., are looked upon as "checks" when in fact they are coordinates, able to be adjusted to produce any desired result.

The coordinates governing these preliminaries so fill the head before the clubhead has moved an inch that others that govern the swing itself are scarcely given a thought. A player may have enough to get the clubhead pointing to the sky at the horizontal, as it must be made to do. He may even have references to check his backswing plane and the slot for his clubhead at the top. After that, nothing.

With its simple shape and leisurely pace permitting the clubhead to be placed on the correct path every inch of the way, most are able to arrive at a position at the top of the backswing which might be turned into a 250 yard straight shot if only what came next was equally leisurely and clear.

Alas, it is not. Thus the hit is made down any number of paths, not one of which is correct—all bringing the hands and the clubhead to be laterally to the front far too soon and none of which will ever bring the top assembly down to the only position from which a correct release of the clubhead can be made.

Most golfers who can actually play to a handicap of between 14 and 24 have long ago settled on the least destructive—for them—of these paths, but it is still the wrong path with a built-in release inhibitor common to all wrong paths. Despite full fitness and physique their shots seem always lacking in real power.

Those who swing their clubhead to their front with a three-foot discrepancy between the incorrect and the cor-

rect position will have the higher handicaps. Handicaps reduce in direct ratio to that discrepancy. When the discrepancy is zero, behold, the single figure golfer whose handicap then depends solely upon practice, fine-tuning, and his ability to hole putts.

The bringing of the clubhead into powerful release rests upon bringing the top assembly to its crucial position at the right hip.

It is the expert's primary coordinate, producing both length and repeatability, the fulcrum from which he releases the clubhead from way behind him and higher than his head to explode through the ball with such speed and power that further coordinates from fulcrum to follow-through can only be subliminal.

Dreams, almost. Sensations of the passage of an invisible clubhead pulled down by a straight left arm and cocked right elbow and wrists, below and past the right shoulder to flash from being laterally behind the hands, then under them, or so it seems; on through the ball pulling right arm and club shaft to full extension horizontal to the ground as release melds into follow-through.

As no two golfers are alike, coordinates must be peculiar to the individual, each having as few or as many as he feels are required to produce a satisfactory result and to continuously repeat it. To be measurable, changes made to coordinates when fine-tuning a sound swing should be made little by little.

In changing the locus of a poor swing, far best to start with a clean sweep. Use weight transfer and correctly guided hands to bring the top assembly down. Adjust the cock and set of the wrists, right elbow, and hands until the clubhead exits to the front correctly at about the level of the right knee. When satisfied that you know where the clubhead is throughout the hitting stroke and that you have the coordinates to repeat it, write them down. When changed, write that down, too.

All golfers can learn from Harvey Penick's noting down of each salient point, the better to help a pupil. Ben Hogan also took notes after practice, the better to help his game.

Once, on being introduced as the world's greatest golfer, he made a modest yet profound reply. "Oh, no," he said, "I have often been beaten by much better players than me. Their trouble was that they didn't know why."

The Invisible Lines

With a clear understanding of the paths that a clubhead must be made to follow and a knowledge of coordinates to ensure repetition, it could be argued that to bother with a description of a much older aid to swinging golf clubs might be superfluous. That is not so.

What we know with some certainty is that the ratio of high handicap golfers to card-carrying tournament pros is double that of 70 years ago. Therefore, to bring anything that might be helpful to their attention is surely to be welcomed.

In all probability, the idea of using an imaginary line as an aid was first introduced in an attempt to urge upon an inveterate slicer the necessity of keeping everything on his side of the ball as he swung his golf club.

The original idea was perhaps to help the pupil to understand that the head of the golf club must never be allowed to get on the far side of an imaginary straight line running from the target—not necessarily the flagstick—through the ball and continuing on to infinity. Throughout the stroke the clubhead must not cross that line at ground level or any other level until the ball is on its way—not even then if it can possibly be helped.

Awareness of the imaginary line can be of considerable assistance to any golfer plagued with hitting from the top. There is no doubt that it can provide a valuable mental picture that should give the player a better idea of the paths on which he must swing the clubhead. As he does so he can rid himself of his personal contortions

The use of imaginary lines can help many aspects of the set-up and golf swing.

that never produced anything in the way of a correctly struck ball and bring his movements much nearer to the real thing.

The hope must be that swinging more correctly may rekindle his interest in mastering weight transfer and the first move down from the top, which would, of course, solve everything permanently.

If he does not get that far, some awareness of the invisible line can only improve matters. However, it will always remain a means of improvement with no attention having been paid to the underlying cause of the difficulty. This is what Harvey Penick aptly called "just a sticking plaster cure."

Temporary cure or not, the imaginary line ("the magic line" as Bobby Jones dubbed it) has been in service now for well over a hundred years, proving to be a useful repair outfit for chronic slicers and an instant check for a better player who senses that his swing is beginning to "lose it." If the use of a mental image can do anything at all to give a beginner some sort of feel for the swing it is only to be encouraged. Confidence in a feeling can break the well-known barrier of near paralysis at address that is born of ignorance of rogue elements three and four.

In all probability, the imaginary line was at the root of J. Douglas Edgar's "Gate to Golf" device that was described in an earlier chapter and reported to be extremely effective. The "gate," however, was a tangible device whereas we are evaluating mental images. There are many of them and all may afford some help if properly studied. Most notable is Ben Hogan's imaginary pane of glass, resting on the player's side of the golf ball at its lower edge and then on the player's shoulders, having thrust his head through a large imaginary hole in the middle.

Wonderfully well depicted in his book and a boon to any who may be struggling to find the optimum plane for his backswing, it also offers a perfect image of the lower path of the hitting stroke, together with an explanation of the changed direction of that path. Due to the transfer of weight and the first move down, it clearly shows that the path, now correctly in to out, aims slightly right of the target.

These are splendid images that, as Hogan explained, quickly become unnecessary once the correct moves are integrated within the swing.

Eventually the idea of an invisible line to keep the club from cutting across the ball was further developed to include a line across the shoulders and another across the hips, both parallel with the original imaginary target line. At first a mental picture of the shoulder line does not come easily. However, when looked at from the player's left or right side with his arms hanging almost straight down, its value becomes clearer. The shoulders should be turned fully on either swing path without them getting nearer to the ball.

The least considered of the parallel lines is that which

runs across the extremities of the pelvis (the hips). Least considered the hip line may be, but it is by far the most useful of the imaginary lines to anyone in the process of rebuilding his swing, even more so to a player at peace with his long game, but who suddenly finds himself unable to get down in two from just off the green.

Remember that in his aside to Peter Alliss, Henry Longhurst summed it up in just two lines:

If as we swing we pay more attention to the parts that do not move at all, or move only very little, might we not better control the parts which do?

We have come to believe religiously that the right ear hole does not move at all. We must now consider the extremities of the pelvis (the hips). They are the first of two vital parts within the integral swing which move only very little, far less in fact than a player might imagine, that is if he has thought of it at all. (The final part that moves far less than one might think is the right shoulder, which will be dealt with in a later chapter.)

In an ideal swing, as the club goes to the top, the hips should turn approximately 40 degrees to the shoulders' 90 degrees. The feeling is one of turning the left hip more across than to the front as the player makes a well-centered coil taking the clubhead to the top on its back-swing path.

The hitting stroke (or downswing) is a lower path than that of the backswing, made so by the player trans-ferring the weight below the waist laterally to the left foot while the position of the head and upper body re-mains unchanged in its vertical plane. The lateral move-ment of the hips to the left should be just sufficient to plant the left heel back to the ground and lift the right heel from it, although many fine players swing without lifting the left heel at all.

This movement is quite easily made without a golf club and the more often a player exercises it the better. It is possible that some readers may have already left their chairs to try it. They will have discovered that, with the weight firmly on the right foot when the hands are at the top, the player can do exactly as he wishes with his hands, arms, and shoulders while making no movement of his hips whatsoever.

This ability to move the upper assembly so easily in any direction has been the bane of all who ever failed to play good golf.

The trialist will also have discovered that if the head and upper torso are held properly centered—as they must be throughout—the shoulders/arms/hands assembly at the top is forced into movement as the hips slide left and the waist begins to uncoil. He cannot help himself. If he is to stay well centered the assembly simply has to move. The vital question is: where to?

As Bobby Jones observed, "This is the move which always trips them." It is this move made incorrectly which ruins millions of golf shots every single day.

Let us assume that the novice or high handicap player was facing a wall when he stood to make his exploratory movement of the hips. It is 40,000 to 1 that before his hips had moved six inches to the left (on the downswing), his left arm, his hands, his cocked right elbow assembly, and his right shoulder were all nearer to the wall than they were the moment before he began to move his hips to the left.

If so he has just demonstrated a perfect hit from the top and has almost certainly commenced his usual power-sapping sway to the left.

Interesting though all of this may be, we are digressing. It is not the purpose here to describe the weight transfer or the first move down. That will follow in another chapter. The purpose here is to stress use, and value of, the imaginary parallel lines that, if properly observed, will give the player no end of help when it comes to getting the two rogue elements (the shifting of some of the weight to the left foot and leg and the correct first movement of the hands as the swing changes direction) right.

In transferring the weight the imaginary line across the hips can help in this way. As the left hip moves rapidly to the left and to the rear, the right hip moves to the left across the position it occupied at address. As it slides leftward it may graze its parallel line, but the player should feel quite definitely that it has not crossed it.

Dependent to some extent on the player's girth, from the position at the top to the position at impact neither hip will have traveled more than 12 inches, but they have traveled lightning fast. If they have not, they should have done. It is the speed with which the transfer is made over so little distance that puts rogue element three (the shifting of some of the weight to the left foot and leg) in the split second category and makes it so difficult to clarify.

Before we leave the usefulness of the invisible parallel lines there is one further image seldom, if ever, considered. The knees play a subsidiary but nevertheless significant role in the integral swing. Under control they supply balance, rhythm, and good style. Uncontrolled they make all manner of mischief.

To a swing rebuilder short on knowledge of just where they should and should not go, the parallel line to be borne in mind is that which runs across the toes of the shoes. As the knees respond to the swing, both going up and coming down, neither should be permitted to cross that line.

That piece of advice was tucked away among many descriptions of facets of the swing presented as a series of instructional strips in a national newspaper. The author was noted golf instructor David Leadbetter. For some extraordinary reason many players suffer from an uncontrollable amount of knee movement, the most destructive being a shooting out of the left knee early in the backswing to end up beyond the left toe, leaving nothing to transfer leftward to initiate the first move down.

On the backswing the left knee must turn in toward the toe of the right shoe, from whence its smooth move leftward as the trunk uncoils will pull an unchanged top assembly down to the waist, as it should.

Golfers with a shooting left knee would do well to remember Leadbetter's advice.

7

Think Locus—Never Arc

locus: The exact path traced out by a point moving in
accordance with a defined condition. Plural: loci
Modern University Dictionary

arc: Part of any curve (unfixed). Plural: arcs
Oxford Dictionary

Some years ago, by dint of extremely clever photography, it was possible to study the loci of clubheads as swung by many of the world's great players.

Neither slow motion film nor still swing sequences
has since come close to providing the duffer with such a
precise conception of what the basic fundamentals properly applied will produce for any golfer.

Each photograph was presented as a jet-black rect-
angle so dark that very little of the player or his equipment was discernible. What could be seen and studied,
however, were the loci of the clubhead as it moved along
the upper locus to the top, and then along the lower locus

through release, impact, and follow-through to a classic finish.

The loci appeared as if formed by the flight of a fire-fly, making it abundantly clear that the backswing and the hitting stroke each had its own quite separate locus.

When printed in twos and threes, these pictures of-fered a fascinating comparison of top players' swings showing wide differences in planes, pivots, and the points where the swings changed direction at the very top of each individual's upper locus. From there on, however, despite all manner of differences in players' ages and physical characteristics, a correct weight transfer and first move down of the hands produced almost identical loci in the hitting stroke of each man.

In every case the flight of the firefly traced out a near identical locus to the ball, delivering the clubhead from inside to out. They also demonstrated inside to square to inside. Even the loci for deliberate fades and draws.

Few swings of inferior players seem to have been photographed and published, which is a great pity. In this way a pupil could have used the system to under-stand all that must be changed in his swing and to moni-tor progress until the swing was right.

The reason for this wonderful photography being

discontinued could well have been cost, because it was soon to give way to video. Though video is commendable, it has never produced a picture of the loci of swings as firefly photography could.

While firefly photography was available it was unfortunate that no one thought to take similar photographs of the loci of the hips and other moving parts of an expert player's anatomy. If they had done so, the novice, now fully aware that he must swing the clubhead along two differing but fully defined paths, would also have seen that the locus of the hips on the backswing was not simply reversed on the hitting stroke.

Here again the hips would have been shown to move along two slightly differing loci, the latter locus being prompted by the transfer of the weight below the waist to the left foot and leg.

At this point there may be many readers who have come to realize that the arc of the hitting stroke does not roughly retrace the arc of the backswing as they might previously have thought. Also that the locus of the hips as they pivot is not that which they follow as the hit is made.

To many readers this may have come as something of a shock. There will be skepticism, even disbelief. It would be strange if there is not, for it must question all that they have been striving to do perhaps for several years. Some will be surprised to have read that they have missed just a couple of facts, but facts which contribute so much to the primary objective of every average golfer wishing to improve his game and lower his handicap.

It is amazing that so many millions can be in love with golf for so long yet continue to have so little idea of the shape of the thing they wish their movements to produce. This buttonhole was missed and they are left only with thoughts of some nebulous arc that must be worked upon.

With the cat now out of the bag, any disenchanted golfer prepared to give improvement one more try cannot go far wrong if he makes his start by dispensing with all thoughts of his arc or even of his arcs plural, focusing on his locus and loci.

An arc is part of a curve and all arcs are unfixed in their position. That definition may be a good description of millions of golf swings, but the word arc should play no part in fixing a golfer's mind on precisely how and where he must swing his clubhead.

A locus is the "the exact path traced out by a point moving in accordance with a defined condition," a perfect description of the head of any golf club being swung in the hands of an expert player.

The basic paths of the clubhead for the backswing and
downswing.

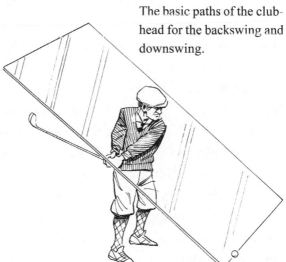

Locus, arc: both such little words—one precise, the other imprecise. In Latin locus means "a precise place or path." With nothing in this world calling for greater precision than the path of a clubhead on its way to a ball, all golfers would do well to adopt the word to fix precisely in their minds their prime objective in every swing they ever make.

Remember, the many stationary preliminaries must be right and can be put right quite easily, but right or wrong they do not hit the ball. The ball is hit by swinging the clubhead up a precise locus to the top, and down a second precise locus through the ball.

No amount of correctness in all of the preliminaries will produce anything in the way of a shot if the swing itself lacks all precision in these two essentials.

British golf in particular has suffered badly from overemphasis on the preliminaries to the detriment of the hitting stroke. Deceived by the old adage—still in use today—that "if it's straight enough, it's far enough."

The American attitude was always very different. It was "first learn to hit it long, then learn to hit it straight." As far back as Jack Burke Sr., all emphasis in America was on the exact locus of the clubhead on the hitting stroke. This was to give America 50 years of golfing domination while elsewhere the game dreamed on.

The purpose of all of this has been to acquaint poor players with the reasons underlying their condition. To question why it should require 40,000 of them to produce one card-carrying tournament professional. To challenge the received wisdom that those tournament professionals play an altogether different game. They do not.

It is simply that the millions who believe that there is one game for them and another for the pros have not begun to understand the reason why these experts are able to play as they do—sometimes despite serious physical handicap or chronic poor health.

Average golfers will only come to return gross scores of 80 or better by dismissing the minutiae that fills their minds covering everything under the sun except the hitting of the ball, by ceasing futile practice which has yet to produce a proper shot, save by the purest accident, and by acquiring an understanding and application of a couple of things that simply must be done correctly.

Which, in truth, is all that master golfers do.

The mysterious two rogues (shifting of some of the weight to the left foot and leg and the correct first movement of the hands as the swing changes direction) will be enlarged upon in the next chapter. Though they are individual facets, just, thinking of them as such is bound to result in jerkiness. The swing is a harmony of movement into which the two rogues blend to make an integral whole. When all is correct and fully blended, harmony of movement not only becomes easy but inevitable, providing rhythm, smooth acceleration, and power below the waist where it really matters.

It will also have stylish aggression as the clubhead is released through the ball at maximum speed—a hallmark of all superior players.

With the two rogues tamed, a powerful release is the easiest move in golf, a final reflex requiring no thought on the part of the player.

Release must be always total. There is no such thing as a partial release in any shape or form. A clubhead can only be properly released if it has been drawn, solely by the weight transfer, down along its correct locus, still well behind the player when the hands are just above the waist. The fully cocked right elbow assembly and wrists having not yet released a smidgen of their stored-up power.

This vital swing position simply screams for release, which drags the clubhead down to exit laterally to the front of the player somewhere about the level of the right knee and on along a low angle of attack through the ball.

The plain fact unlearned by millions is that if they

are without knowledge of the correct weight transfer and a properly directed first move down, they can never lower the shoulders/arms/hands assembly into that vital spot.

Without that knowledge they are forever forced to expend their power somewhere above their shoulders—often above their heads—and at the ball find that they have little left to hit with. What is left is a snatchy spin of the shoulders and torso in an attempt to give some sort of propulsion to a clubhead that is decelerating and two or three feet off track.

They must be content with this weakness of impact. In such a swing, the weaker the impact, the better. Any attempt at a total release of a clubhead not remotely close to its correct lower locus can only end in tears.

Again we digress. It was not the intention to drift from urging the golfer to cease all thought of a nebulous and variable arc in favor of the much more definite locus, onto the mention of release which will be touched upon again when discussing the swing in its entirety. Nevertheless, its mention at this stage will not have been misplaced if it impresses upon the poorer player this greatest of all the benefits to accrue from learning the correct transfer and start-down.

In actual fact there is little that can be written of release. One can only write of the vital position from which release is made. Release is a subliminal perception, oc-curring at lightning speed and without awareness or de-liberation. Release cannot be seen and thus is not described, but it can most certainly be heard.

At great championships, any who has stood around a teeing ground will remember all their lives the sounds generated by the practice swings of the stars as they lim-bered up for the next full drive. What can possibly be written to describe the awesome swish that is release? Nothing is ever seen of it and the golfer seemed scarcely to move.

Release such as this is lightning acceleration, low down along a precise locus.

To warn once more: The stationary preliminaries and vital moves within the swing can all be properly done, but if there is the slightest sway of the right ear to the left the shot will be spoiled and all style will vanish com-pletely.

8

The Swing

The Importance of the Pivot

A golf ball can only be struck correctly by use of a harmonious and rhythmical swinging of the clubhead, within which four basic elements must be fully integrated.

1. A steady head and upper torso, positioned well behind the ball, where they remain until the ball is struck.
2. A thorough knowledge of the two paths along which the clubhead must be swung.
3. The correct transfer of some of the weight to the left leg.
4. A properly directed first move down from the top that puts the clubhead on its correct lower locus to the ball.

The above may have been what Walter Hagen would have had in mind when he said, "Everything I know about golf could easily be written on a postcard."

As just demonstrated, so it can be, but Hagen's quip failed to deal with one great difficulty. That is the time lapse between an aspiring player's introduction to the game and his assimilation of the few essentials written on the postcard.

If a beginner from day one is fortunate enough to have a teacher determined to hammer in the above fundamentals, there is an excellent chance that the novice will go on to play single figure golf.

For the millions less fortunate in the quality of their instruction, those who have been lazy in the use of it, and those who have sought no instruction at all, any change from worse to better is quite a different matter.

With the average golfer, the lapse of time between his taking up the game and becoming acquainted with the basic essentials of the swing can be anything from a single season to many seasons to never. If and when enlightenment should arrive, he must be prepared to change well-ingrained bad habits, which is never easy.

When working with virgin material the perseverance of a good teacher can quickly do the trick, but the changing of a faulty swing that has been long in use requires a considerable act of will on the part of the player. Given the will, it is not too difficult if for the first time in his golfing life he has in his head a prior knowledge of exactly what it is he is trying to do.

The good news is that none of the four basic elements that make for a correctly struck shot is in any way dependent upon the strength of the player. The still right ear. Concentration upon the loci. Weight transfer and the start down are all matters of knowledge and technique that require little force.

What weight transfer and start down do require is time and room to make them. The time and room needed are supplied by means of a full pivot, these days called "completion of the backswing."

Any swing rebuilder attempting to get weight transfer and start down correct without maximizing the time and space he gives himself in which to do it is certain to suffer disappointment and frustration. Neither move can be made effectively in a quick, snatchy, and cramped condition.

Quick, cramped swings are almost universal among high handicap golfers, but none of them is impervious to change. Generally they are the result of a player having allowed his pivot to ossify over many seasons of trying to keep his ball in the fairway. When a player is forced to inhibit his swing as his only means of hanging on to any vestige of good form, the completion of the backswing is the first thing to be sacrificed.

Never certain of precisely what he should do at the top, he has found that a full pivot adds nothing but further trouble. He very soon lapses into what he finds to be a more controllable three-quarter swing, unconsciously waving goodbye to any opportunity to play really good golf.

Properly executed, weight transfer and good clubhead control on the lower locus to the ball can, of course, be applied to a three-quarter or even a half-swing. This is well demonstrated by those players—and there are many of them—still able to get it round in a gross score that is less than their age. It also explains the success of those who have played at a high level with some serious physical incapacity.

Nevertheless, the more difficult job of operating the basic elements within a truncated swing is most definitely not for the player with half his golfing days still before him. Swing rebuilders without the excuse of age or infirmity, but who have settled on making less than a full pivot, would do well to start by improving their ability to turn their shoulders.

Some readers will give up at this point having come

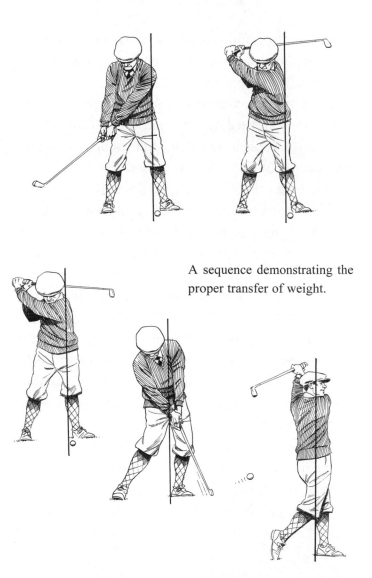

A sequence demonstrating the proper transfer of weight.

to believe that a full turn of the torso is beyond them. This is not the case. There is a very simple exercise that will quickly restore a neglected pivot, provided that the rebuilder has no muscular/skeletal condition that might be adversely affected by increased effort. Those that do must recognize their incapacity and continue with their three-quarter or half-swing as before.

The player should stand in a right-angled corner of a room facing one wall with another wall at his left shoulder. Taking grip of an imaginary club, stretch out the arms until the hands are about waist height. With the head held well centered and with the right ear motionless, turn the upper torso until the back is fully facing the wall on the left.

Take it very gently for the first few days, but discipline yourself to do it regularly. It will do two things for you: (1) it will help you create a full pivot, and (2) it will help you learn to keep the right ear completely still while the turn is made.

After a few days take up the address position instead of standing erect. Make a fully completed backswing, checking that the shoulders have turned their full 90 degrees to be parallel with the wall. Done religiously this exercise will quickly restore the muscles of a torso, stiff from lack of use. Once toned up and used correctly in a full pivot, these muscles will add power to any swing.

The completion of the backswing has great importance to any golfer who is conversant or about to become conversant with basic elements three and four. Through practice, he will quickly realize that unless he completes it he will have neither the time nor the room to execute these vital movements correctly.

Persevere with this. It is the only extra physical effort required within a swing rebuild. It is a curious fact that an ineffective swing has always required greater effort in its operation than an effective one. Effectiveness is simply knowledge and applied technique. Both should be effortless and almost painless.

Many readers, having checked on the four basic elements, will have questioned the omission of the moves that follow impact. They are part of the swing are they not? The reason is because the ball is already on its way when they enter the picture and nothing can influence it further. For the moment, the through swing (latter part of release) and the follow-through are best grouped with the preliminaries.

They will be looked at later. Both are utterly dependent upon the basics between start back and impact having been executed correctly. It cannot be the other way around. If the basics are right, the latter part of release and follow-through simply confirm the fact.

Look upon the through swing and classic finish as a sort of afterglow, simply to be enjoyed when all else has been right. We have followed Tommy Armour's advice. Having dumped the wretched maze of detail, our business now is to learn and hammer in his two or three essentials. A maypole finish to his swing has never yet concerned a golfer still in ignorance of them.

Having earlier questioned the effectiveness of teaching the game in strict sequence from grip to follow-through, it might well be asked why weight transfer and start down cannot be dealt with here and now?

It would be a fair question, but a golf swing is a single harmonious movement in which weight transfer and start down must be made to blend.

It is difficult to find any description of the actual swinging of the club in which the instructor or author fails to warn against the danger of thinking of the swing as a series of individual movements. Such a fragmented interpretation can all too easily replace the concept of fluid motion with the kind of jerkiness to be seen on every golf course. The swing is the thing. In the player's mind, swinging the clubhead smoothly through its loci must always be greater than any of the swing's several parts.

There is also the problem one meets in every kind of sporting pursuit. If you wish to excel, should you play the game to get fit or first get fit to play the game? Effective golf depends upon the player applying the fullest pivot that his age and physical makeup makes available to him. The importance of this cannot be overstated. It has already been described and an exercise to restore an unresponsive torso recommended.

The Backswing

The function of the backswing is to swing the clubhead as smoothly as possible to the most advantageous point from which to change its direction downward and as nearly as possible to repeat the process in each and every swing. The point at which the direction is made to change must be sufficiently far back to allow time and space for the change to be made effectively.

When a hacker bemoans the vagaries that beset his game, the astonishing thing is that he seldom attributes any of them to problems within his backswing. A duffer's swing is of his own manufacture and as such, he should know it intimately. Nevertheless, in every round he plays he must iron out the vagary of the day. In attempting to do so he may well play using 30 different backswings.

Knowing nothing of what he should do as the clubhead changes direction, he is left with the notion that it should be swung in an arc to the top by means of a straight left arm and a cocking of the wrists. He believes that there are several arcs available to him. On any given day he will vary them in an attempt to get more length or loft or to correct faults that have resulted in misdirected shots.

He may be aware that a wide arc is considered to be best, but if timing goes, as it often seems to do, he may narrow it a little. It can be made steep or deep or shallow. He can try his extended arc or his foreshortened arc. It can be upright or flat or a dozen settings in between.

He has built the most functional swing of which he is capable, but each round still calls for some adjustment. Despite it all, no amount of play or practice has resulted in improved scores or handicap.

Most such swings have been built in the absence of knowledge of any better way. For the swing rebuilder the first step to a better way must be taken by obtaining the clearest possible understanding of the function of the backswing. His second step is to learn precisely what happens next.

With the exception of changes forced upon him by most bunker shots and occasional awkward lies, an expert player's standard backswing for shots requiring full power has been made as constant as it is possible for him to do. This is "grooving." His object is to swing the clubhead along its locus to the top with him as steady as a rock beneath it—still perfectly centered, and having sufficient time to start the clubhead smoothly down along its lower locus to the ball.

The preliminaries are complete. The first of his four basics, a steady head, is positioned well behind the ball where it is anchored by the still right ear. There will be the odd mannerism personal to every player, but the indecision seen at address in most average players is totally absent, replaced by basic element number two: concentration upon the paths along which he is about to swing the clubhead.

Low and slow, he starts it back along a line straight back from the ball. The triangle formed by shoulders, arms, and hands move away in one piece. When the clubhead has traveled a foot or so it is made to turn inside the invisible line and also to rise by the turning of his shoulders and torso around his angled yet perfectly centered spine.

When his straight left arm has reached the horizontal, the right elbow has begun to fold and together with the wrists will be fully cocked when his hands and arms reach their highest point, placing the clubhead at the very end of its backswing locus. He has completed his backswing smoothly, even slowly, though it has taken little more than a second.

The exact path of the clubhead as defined by the player is its locus. He fixes this locus by the use of two coordinates: (1) The radius of his straight left arm turning as a gyro around a perfectly centered spine, and (2) the top anchor secured by a motionless right ear. By definition all loci are fixed and by the use of coordinates can be constantly repeated. The clubhead is now at the determined point where the expert will change its direction and accelerate it smoothly down a lower locus to arrive at the ball as it reaches its maximum speed.

In his book, Ben Hogan wrote of his total concentration on swinging his clubhead "along a set slot (locus) throughout my backswing. If I did that the clubhead was bound to hit the point at the head of the slot on swing after swing after swing."

This is the repeating swing so admired and so desired by all ambitious golfers. It is a thing of the greatest geometrical beauty, so fixed in its coordinates that the touring professional can literally hit the ball time after time with his eyes shut.

With the aid of a friend simply to assist with direction and the placing of the clubhead to the ball, by use of his personal loci and coordinates, so too can a blind golfer. So too can any player prepared to work hard to get his loci right.

So near and yet so far have millions been. In one choice of words or another, the way to a repeating and powerful swing has been explained by teachers and otherwise described in many thousands of publications. Bobby Jones felt that "most average golfers swing to the top with fair success." Yet the inability of so many of them to master the next step leads to all consistency in the backswing being abandoned.

Once a player wittingly or unwittingly reduces his pivot to better control problems induced by a faulty change of direction, his handicap can never be much better than 20.

Because players differ greatly in age and physical makeup, the locus of any backswing is unique to its owner. Yet if each is arrived at by the application of simple geometry and sound coordinates, all will be equally valid—each consistently able to position the clubhead to set up a correct pass at the ball, swing after swing after swing.

While it is true that players with unorthodox swings have won great championships, any novice just starting out or a high handicapper in the process of rebuilding is well advised to use the orthodox swing as a model when fashioning or refashioning his own. Orthodox swings are still in the great majority.

There is nothing difficult in starting the clubhead back low and slow for the first foot or so. Remembering, of course, that it must *not* get outside the invisible line. Is the clubhead pushed away or dragged away? There are advocates of both methods, but the received wisdom is that with the left arm and shaft of the club in a straight line at address, a push of the left hand should predominate.

This method continues to emphasize the straight left arm and makes for good extension at the horizontal when the hands reach waist-height going back.

Pulling or dragging the clubhead away with the right hand at start back, if not closely watched, can lead to the common fault of picking up the club as opposed to swinging it. Many swing rebuilders will have suffered this fault in their old swings. It is most commonly caused by abandoning the pivot and adopting a simpler but less effective backswing. This is a further reason to recommend that a pushing pressure by the left hand, arm, and shoulder should start the clubhead back.

That is not to say that the right hand should be completely passive at this stage. In his instructional articles in *Golf Monthly* magazine, Greg Norman advocates the feeling of stretching out the right hand as the clubhead is taken back "as if to shake hands with a friend standing to the player's right."

This is not just a good notion, but also one that works like a charm. It is an excellent aid in starting the swing and in getting it to full extension. It supplies a strong sense of the hands working in unison. At the horizontal, it can also be of assistance in making sure that the tip of the clubhead points directly to the heavens, as it should.

In a perfectly centered pivot, it is at and beyond the horizontal that pressure is felt in the right leg as it correctly resists the turning of the torso.

Many years ago another well-respected contributor to *Golf Monthly* magazine—who wrote under the name of "Mr. X"—produced a number of durable little cards on instruction. One of these extolled the virtue of what he called the "right shin post." The shin post was the right lower leg from knee to foot that, he advised, must soak up the pressure of the turn with no movement whatsoever until the direction of the swing was about to change. This is yet another instance of the value of a part remaining completely stationary, albeit this time only throughout the backswing.

Today it is recommended that the pressure be absorbed by the inside muscles of the right leg and the weight taken on the inside of the right foot and heel. This sounds plausible and may well do the job, but Mr. X's idea of the right shin post is still very much a contender. What is certain is, that to stay well centered as the golfer must, then the turn should be resisted in some manner. If it is not, the right knee may buckle or the whole body may sway to the right and take the head with it. Each can be equally disastrous.

If all is right at the horizontal. If the left arm is straight, if we are shaking hands with a friend and the clubhead points directly to the sky, then the player is on course for swinging on plane.

There is no better description of the importance of the planes than Ben Hogan's pane of glass or Tony Jacklin's bicycle wheel, outlined in their respective books. Any player having problems with the planes of his swing would benefit greatly from reading both if he can find them.

As a quick reminder, a golfer's true planes are defined by an imaginary line from the ball, through the nape of the neck and on up to infinity. The thing to be remembered is that the planes must be made to change with the clubhead's change of direction. No great damage is done by swinging a little beneath them. However, if either the hands or the clubhead get above either plane, the shot will almost certainly be spoiled.

Generally, at the top, a left arm lying near the right ear is probably overly upright – and seems about to burst through the backswing plane if it has not already done so. A left arm lying below the right shoulder can be said to be overly flat. In bringing either of these extremes of plane to the ball, compensation is almost certain to be needed elsewhere on the way down. Only a few can cope with such unnecessary additional pressure.

To repeat, if all is right at the horizontal, within any limit imposed by age, turn the torso as fully as possible and swing the clubhead to the top by bringing the straight left arm somewhere adjacent to the center of the right collarbone.

As you commence to strike the ball more nearly correctly, some fine adjustment of the backswing plane may be required. That done, you will have found your personal backswing locus. It will be unique to you and you must stick to it for all full shots.

Remember, the great beauty of a locus is that it cannot be other than fixed. The arc you have just abandoned can be anything at all. Never return to it. Your backswing locus will place the clubhead repeatedly on the point at which a correct weight transfer and start down can be made and with sufficient room and time in which to make them. It is something you have almost certainly never enjoyed before.

Much as one dislikes leaving the positive aspects of the game to mention the negative, it may be helpful to the swing rebuilder to recognize some damaging faults to be avoided when attempting to groove a new backswing.

Putting the clubhead outside the invisible line in the first couple of feet going back is one. Crossing the invisible line very early coming down is even worse, for the stroke must now be completed with no downswing plane whatsoever. Both of these should be taken care of when the first move down is fully understood.

Since this first move down is the devil that condemns millions to high handicaps, we will say no more about him in this subchapter in the hope that he may be exorcised in the next.

Another serious fault already touched upon is "picking up the club" as opposed to swinging the clubhead. This one seldom troubles beginners, who are more often to be seen extending for dear life in an effort to hit it long. Picking up the club is a fault that is born as the rogue elements are encountered, go unlearned, and all hope of single figures disappears. It is here that the player shortens sail in an effort to keep the ball in play, losing all vestige of real power in the process.

By making the whole thing smaller he feels he is reducing his margin for error, which it almost always does. The player then begins a life of patting it down the middle en route to a six. Power will not return to his stroke until he ceases to pick up the club with little or no pivot and turning fully, swings it to the top through the most extended locus available to him.

Finally, there is a less common fault that could well afflict a swing rebuilder and therefore must be worth mentioning. He has just dismantled his inferior swing and is now tangling with invisible lines, full extension, right shin posts, etc. It is inevitable that he will often check on the position of his clubhead as he holds it at various stages on its new backswing locus.

Professional teachers call this "watching the club back." There is general agreement among instructors that it should be avoided. They say it can become habitual, though one might spend a lifetime on golf courses and never come across a serious case of it.

Swing rebuilding may be just the occupation in which it can be used sparingly. Particularly if it helps to get the rebuilder going, improves his grasp of what it is he is trying to do, and pumps confidence into his practice. After all, most professional teachers regularly call upon their pupils to make checks on the clubhead at the horizontal and at the top. They cannot hope to have it both ways.

Nevertheless, "watching it back" is said to be a destructive habit to acquire, so the advice is this: As soon as you know where the clubhead is, watch it no more. Until then do anything you must to get to know exactly where it is both going up and coming down until you have absolute confidence in the loci and coordinates of your rebuilt backswing.

At the Top

There was a time when the optimum slot for the clubhead at the top was so well defined that, having arrived there, pupils were urged by their teachers to pause before changing direction downward. The fact that the pause at the top was an ancient technique used to assist in the swinging of hickory-shafted clubs is of no consequence. It continues to demonstrate the emphasis that should be given to the position at the top and to the vital importance of what comes next, for what comes next is the most crucial part of the swing.

A pause at the top is seldom to be seen today and it is fairly safe to say that it is never heard as a definite instruction from a professional teacher, except perhaps as an aid to correcting a faulty rhythm. The pause died—a casualty of technological progress—with the advent of the steel shaft and subsequent birth of "the power swing."

Lost with the pause was the brief moment it allowed the player to get the change of direction and the lower locus of the hitting stroke right.

It was no accident that in the first 30 years of steel shafted clubs the greatest exponents of golf were a 50-50 mix of both amateur and professional players who had all been weaned on hickory.

It is at the very beginning of the downswing that the shot is made or marred. When at the top, it is in the execution of what comes next that the single-figure player and the average golfer part company. This is reason enough for the high handicap player to do nothing further with his game until he possesses a complete and unambiguous understanding of the transfer of some of his weight and the first move down of the shoulders/arms/hands assembly. It is these and only these that will produce the locus to bring the clubhead laterally to the front of him at knee height or thereabouts.

Instructional literature and videos these days are unlikely to provide much of real assistance in this area. Weight transfer and the first move down may be touched upon, but will seldom be substantive.

In all probability the reason for the dearth of information on these two awkward essentials of the swing lies in difficulty with their description. The teacher, demonstrator, or author is called upon to find words for a complexity of both passive and active movement that takes place in a flash. Bitter experience of years of failure may also play a part, though this should never be an excuse for lack of perseverance in the teacher or the pupil.

So where does all this leave a swing rebuilder or a novice seriously bent upon improvement?

He can do no better than to book a series of lessons with a good teaching professional, immediately declaring his determination to learn to swing the clubhead along its correct lower path to the ball. He should request a check that his position at the top is the best that his physical ability will allow and make clear his desire to learn, really learn to exit the clubhead to his front at knee height and not waist height or shoulder height.

That is to say the correct transfer of the weight below his waist to his left leg and the correct first move down of his shoulders/arms/hands assembly to the exclusion of all else. When these are right, for the first time in his golfing life and with no further thought on his part, he will experience the correct release of the clubhead.

These three things are all that govern the path of the clubhead from its optimum slot at the top to its correct delivery through the ball. The last of these three—release—is the element that provides maximum speed at impact.

With these correct, what happens after impact—the completion of release and the classic follow-through—cannot help but take care of themselves, requiring nothing at all from the player.

When booking a series of lessons, detailing the content required is a perfectly proper thing to do. It will be considered neither cheek nor hubris. Every day thousands of hopefuls seek lessons on this or that specific facet of the swing, which the pro is perfectly happy to supply.

When presented with a prospective pupil who admits to knowing nothing of the change of direction and is determined to learn it, the pupil should not be surprised if confirmation of the booking is delayed for some minutes while the pro regains his composure.

Ten half-hour lessons should do it, costing no more than 200 pounds—less if the pupil can obtain a sympathetic deal for a series of lessons during the off-season. In the first two or three lessons the pro may require him to hit few, if any, golf balls. At this stage it is the bringing of the clubhead down from behind him to be level with the right knee or thereabouts that must be his major concern. Despite hitting no balls, 30 minutes will be found to be plenty.

An earlier chapter described the correct employment of the two rogue elements as being comparatively simple and almost painless to learn. Almost painless, for when made correctly beneath a perfectly still right ear, the transferring of the weight below the waist and the subsequent directing of the hands correctly, will engage the large muscle in the right upper back just below the right shoulder blade.

Until toned up, this may be felt somewhat by the more mature player and often by younger men and women who have been unaware of the major part this muscle plays in preventing the most common fault in golf: hitting "from the top" (also known as "casting").

This is because, in the absence of a correct weight transfer, the first move down in all poor swings is a casting of the hands and right shoulder forward to the right front of the player. Spinning out in this manner makes no demand whatsoever on the large muscle of the right upper back.

Hitting from the top is not only a hopeless arc on which to throw the clubhead, but a massive leak of power.

Transferring Some of the Weight and the First Move Down from the Top

As previous passages of this book have already emphasized, these two little rogues come in a sequence so rapid that it can scarcely be measured in microseconds. The dilemma is this: Are they best described as individual facets of the swing (which in fact they are), or dealt with as a single entity (which they most definitely are not)? Either way lays the very danger of misinterpretation and misunderstanding that has plagued teachers and pupils since golf began.

Most professional teachers treat them for what they are, individual movements. This method certainly cements the vital sequence of events. "Shift your weight onto your left side then wallop the ball" is simple enough to follow. However, at the top the shoulders/arms/hands assembly is fully articulated. Left to itself it is free to move in any direction. The trip wire here is the choice of arcs along which to direct the wallop.

Fraught with danger, this is the moment that defeats 75 percent of all who play the game.

Teaching weight transfer and start down as individual movements of the swing makes it almost impossible to keep up with the incredibly fast timing required by the sequence. This usually produces one or other of two types of golfer. The first is the wild man whose rapid transfer but faulty start down produces all manner of misdirected shots. The second type is more nearly correct, but necessarily more hesitant. He does everything right without really hitting the ball. His deliberate stringing of the second move after the first means that the microseconds have become decaseconds, draining his shots of all vitality.

Despite what always appears to be very steady play, he hits every shot that little bit too late to leave him forever wondering just what he must do to find more power. Such gentle players of every age and physique are common to all golf clubs. Unless the decaseconds can be made microseconds, inducing greater speed into the hips, feet, and legs, the condition is irremediable and his handicap will remain in the 20s.

Dealing with these two as a single entity retains the required sense of an almost simultaneous movement, which it almost is—but not quite. Microseconds or not, there is a vital succession that must always be applied. The movement below the waist must initiate—and power—the first movement of the assembly up above.

If this vital sequence becomes reversed, there can be an all-too-easy return to the player hitting hopelessly from the top in the old familiar way. Disenchantment sets in, followed by abandonment of correct weight transfer and a lifetime of being saddled with a high handicap.

There are few aspiring golfers who would not settle for good timing and real power, thus the subtitle dealing with weight transfer and start down amalgamates the two and the good sense of the reader must be relied upon.

As mentioned earlier, Bobby Jones's view was that "most average players advance to the top with fair success, but it is the next step that always trips them." Faced with scores forever in the 90s, it seemed to him ridiculous that their owners should make no attempt to learn "the one or two essential elements which would immediately improve matters."

Ben Hogan's thinking was that "the average golfer's problem is not so much a lack of ability in the playing of the game as it is a lack of knowing exactly what it is that he should do."

In his book, Hogan describes weight transfer and start down as "the most crucial part of the swing, where what a player does either pays off or it doesn't." Forty years later, his description is still the definitive word on these vital fundamentals of good golf.

We cannot know how many golfers who play down to nine or less have benefited from the instruction offered by these and other great players and teachers of an earlier time. It must be a considerable number because since their books were published 50 years ago or more, there seems to have been precious little further on this subject of any real substance. Thus today's player must dig back quite some way to find anything of value.

It is true that, following some notable success, perhaps in a major tournament, a number of "quickie" my-way books by the odd touring professional continue to come through as they have always done. Most do describe the author's method of direction change perfectly well, but generally with insufficient emphasis to alert the reader to the fact that this really is make-or-break time.

For each of these, it is also possible to find hundreds

of instructional books and articles that make no mention of this crucial area of the swing. They may contain literally dozens of quick cures, tips and nostrums, but offer no more than half a dozen lines on weight transfer and none at all on the first move down.

Things could not have been much better in America where, in 1983, Mike Mural Jr. wrote an article for the United States PGA magazine titled "Weight Transfer." This one bright spot in a general dearth of information was reproduced by *Golf Monthly* magazine in June of that year.

Mural's article consisted of three full-page columns with accompanying photographs. It provided the student with an excellent analysis of weight transfer and its critical importance to the swing.

He wrote that weight transfer and the first move down have been vital elements in any efficient golf swing since the game began. He attributed the tremendous gain in swing efficiency in the 1930s to a refinement of those moves that resulted in scores tumbling to below 280 in 72-hole championships.

It was 20 years ago that Mural wrote that even in America "there has not been sufficient emphasis on weight transfer in recent years. Pupils being simply told that it is proper, adds power, and gives the swing a fluid look. Such teaching concepts only scratch the surface."

It is the emphasis on the importance of weight transfer and start down that is so apparent in the writings of
most of those who were there at the change from hickory
to steel.

The fact that after 50 years or more the work of these
American and American émigrés continues to be the best
available on the subject, is that which underpinned the
years of domination enjoyed by United States' golfers
between the wars and for almost 30 years afterward.

At major championships one can spend a week within
10 feet of all the world's great players with the eyes glued
to their hips, or their hands at the top, or both. The odds
are that you will exit no wiser than you entered.

Small wonder then that analysis and description of
this baffling mix of a couple of quite small movements
condemns the vast majority of golfers to mediocrity.

The correct hitting stroke should definitely commence
with a transferring of the weight below the waist to the
left foot and leg (Element Number Three). In many instructional articles this movement is invariably described
as "shifting the weight"—a misnomer that has bred more
misunderstanding and early disenchantment with the
game than anything else. If "shifting the weight" is am-
biguous, then "Let the weight all flow to the left" or "Ev-

erything must move to the left with the shot" can be down-right damaging. In fact it is only some of the weight which is transferred, that below the waist.

As the transfer is made, the upper body and head must retain their position in a vertical plane, remaining well behind the object to be hit.

The movement of the hips to the left should be just enough to plant the left heel firmly to the ground and lift the right heel from it as the weight transfers. Rotation of the hips occurs simultaneously with their small lateral move to the left. The shifting of the weight is not a languid movement. It must be made as fast as possible without destroying rhythm. The feeling must be that, as the hips make their slide-cum-rotation just a few inches to the left, neither has broken the invisible line across them at address.

Remember, the lateral movement to the left can easily be overdone. The fashionable massive hip and knees slide of 25 years ago was short-lived. The threat to the centering of the upper body and head was simply too great, but much misleading literary instruction and photographs of the phenomenon still survive.

When the expert unwinds his hips and trunk correctly, his assembly at the top must also move. It cannot help itself. The direction in which it moves is Element Number Four. The expert's only concern is to control that direction. This is what ensures that the clubhead only takes the path that will produce a correctly struck shot.

Every professional golfer knows that as he changes direction downward, the enforced movement of his shoulders/arms/hands assembly is a secondary movement, powered entirely by the transfer of the weight below his waist onto his left foot and leg, together with a simultaneous unwinding of his hips and trunk.

It is the shifting and unwinding below the waist which supplies all of the force necessary to move the assembly downward—more than enough to bring his arms and hands down from way behind and higher than his head to be level with his waist, but laterally still a shade behind him. Not one moment before they have arrived in this position do the arms or hands turn on any power of their own.

In his inimitable fashion, Lee Trevino once made a profound if cryptic comment on the game generally. "Golf," he said, "is a game played entirely below the waist." It may not be too much to hope that the previous paragraph will help the novice and high handicappers to understand exactly what he meant.

To take these two in sequence, the transfer of the weight comes first. Only just second—but definitely second—comes the correctly guided first movement of the hands as the shoulders/arms/hands assembly is obliged to make a secondary response to the primary force being exerted below the waist.

The paradox is that of these two movements it is the second, the involuntary response of the upper assembly, which is of paramount importance.

As Bobby Jones so beautifully put it, "this is the step which usually trips them." In ignorance of the correct first move of the top assembly, the step they trip on is that irresistible feeling to which all poor golfers are prone—that on arrival at the top they should turn on the power of the shoulders, arms and hands there and then.

With the exception of any player who, from the waist down is made of reinforced concrete, the use of power above the head in such an erroneous and unbalanced fashion will always result in a sway. It will jerk the upper body and the head to the left, throw the hands to the front, and cause the clubhead and several inches of the shaft to cross the invisible line and be laterally to the front of the player while still higher than his shoulders.

Any semblance of a correct stroke is now impossible. Only deceleration and contortion elsewhere will make anything at all of the strike.

It is impossible to overemphasize that it is weight

transfer and the unwinding of the hips that initiates the first movement of the shoulders/arms/hands assembly downward from the top. As it is forced to move the assembly remains virtually unchanged, particularly in respect to the fully cocked wrists and right elbow.

The assembly offers no resistance and supplies no power whatsoever to the move it must make. However, the direction in which it first moves is of critical importance.

Of all the lines of direction made available by the ability of the arms and hands at the top to move wherever they wish, that from the butt end of the rubber grip straight down to the ball is the favorite of millions. It is as destructive as a dozen other equally erroneous lines of direction, all of which carry the hands and clubhead to the front of the player far too early.

Assuming that the backswing has been completed to the best of the player's ability, the direction in which the hands must be guided is exactly that in which the end of the rubber grip is pointing when at the very top of the backswing.

There must be no conscious effort, only guidance in the direction indicated by the butt end of the grip. It should certainly not be pointing at the ball and for the first couple of inches will not necessarily be pointing in a downward direction.

On no account must the butt end be thrown from the top down along a direct line to the ball or anything approaching it.

The alignment of the club shaft at the top is unique to each individual and thus the direction in which the end of the grip points will vary greatly from player to player. For the old, the rotund, and those with osteopathic problems, it may be no farther back than above the right side pocket of the trousers. For the young and supple player it will be way behind him and higher than his head. There will be any number of positions in between.

Whatever the case, provided that the player has turned into the fullest possible pivot, the advice holds true. As the weight below the waist transfers leftward under a vertically fixed right ear and upper body, the first move of the hands should be directed, not powered, exactly in the direction in which the end of the grip is pointing.

For those with a restricted pivot but good wrist cock, this will probably be obliquely downward and a little away from them to their right. As the weight transfer induces the hands to move, this is the direction in which they must be guided.

For all with three-quarter swings, which includes most average golfers, the position is a little less simple; the grip will have gone through its point of fullest extension to be swung up above and behind the player. When it reaches the top, the grip end will be pointing somewhat away from the target. With a good full cock of the wrists it might well be pointing directly away from the target.

How far should the hands continue in the direction indicated by the grip? The answer is roughly the same distance that the right elbow is away from the side when at the top. Usually just two or three inches. In the case of a would-be John Daly swinging well beyond the horizontal, perhaps as much as a foot before dropping downward in the direction of a point somewhat outside the right foot.

Making the first move down of the hands in any other direction than that indicated by the end of the grip will set the clubhead on a dozen erroneous arcs, but never on a locus that will provide a correct pass at the ball time after time after time. The much sought-after dependable repeating swing.

The hips have moved very rapidly. The correctly guided hands have returned the right upper arm and fully cocked right elbow smartly to the player's right side where it, too, has just one correct position. The point of the fully cocked right elbow must be at or fractionally to the right of the player's right hipbone.

The cocked right elbow is now leading the right forearm into the shot. Pregnant with power, not one ounce of it has yet been released. Unless the player has an unusually wide stance, the right thumbnail is now that part of his anatomy farthest from the target.

The hands should be no further to the front than level with the toe of the right shoe, right elbow and wrists still fully cocked and set as to hold the clubhead behind the player and still higher than his head.

The right shoulder has lowered into a position above the right heel. It is from this position, back and down, that the right shoulder becomes the fulcrum for the arms, wrists, and hands to make a fast and total release of the clubhead through and beyond the ball.

Always with the proviso that the backswing has been properly completed, this advice on the first move down will set the top assembly powerfully at the waist—the position that Ben Hogan considered the most important in any golf swing—the most important because it is the only position from which the clubhead can be properly released along a locus to bring it laterally to the front of the player at about the level of the right knee, attacking the ball from the inside, low, square and at maximum speed.

It is of interest to note that a golfer with the knowledge or luck to consistently set the clubhead on a half-decent path to the ball, but who may have abandoned all attempt at transferring his weight, may still hit it off his back foot reasonably well to a handicap of 20 or so. The reverse by no means follows.

A player with good weight transference in his swing, but no idea of the first move down almost always hits from the top. Using any number of the "arcs" that full articulation makes available to him, in a series of powerful wild shots he may somehow work it round the course in less than a hundred strokes, but by no stretch of the imagination can it be said that he did it well.

Release

Release (releasing the clubhead) is one of a dozen currently fashionable expressions designed to give a clearer mental picture of particular aspects of the golf swing.

These have now come to form a "modern" terminology that is steadily replacing golf's ancient nomenclature, much of which has been in use for several hundred years.

Other examples of this modishness are set up, start back, completion, start down, spinning out, and hitting fat—all now in universal use, while pivot, upswing, through stroke, schlaffing, and foozling slip steadily out of usage.

Whether each new term is an improvement on the old is debatable, but release undoubtedly is describing as it does a single function that is taking place through what used to be considered three separate areas: the latter half of the downswing, the old hitting zone, and the through swing. However, descriptions of release seldom make clear that it can only be applied from the correct position at the waist, but neither did the older names for this crucial action that provides all power in the shot.

Some of the examples listed above, together with several more, all concern a golfer who is seeking to arrive at that magical position just above the belt. Until he can arrive there correctly, all thought of release is best left completely out of his program. When he does so he will need no instruction on release that will come to him as the most natural thing in the world.

Any player still unversed in weight transfer and the correct guidance down of the top assembly to the waist is quite unable to set an unpowered clubhead into the precise position from which release begins. Attempting to release with the arms, hands, and clubhead in any other position may be fairly compared with a man who pulls the trigger, lacking all knowledge of how to aim the gun.

The word has a beguiling ring to it. To be told "You're not releasing" seems a softer reproach than "You're not getting your wrists into it!"

Neither of these rebukes will teach the average golfer anything and never will until the two rogues are well and truly learned. Nonetheless, millions will continue to knock it round in level sixes, happy, but deluded in the belief that once found, release will cure whatever ails their swing.

All good players know that weight transfer and the subsequent position of the arms and hands at the waist are the cause of their proficiency at the game. Release is simply the effect: the smooth application of power becoming so fast through the ball as to be beyond human consciousness. Millions believe this to be a quite different game of golf—the one that the experts play, never to be granted to the average golfer. It is no such thing.

In fact, releasing the clubhead could just as profitably be termed "releasing the arms" because it concerns the arms, wrists, and hands every bit as much as the clubhead.

In his excellent "Golf School" articles published in

Golf Monthly magazine, Jack Nicklaus (writing with Ken Bowden) describes this hazy subject as "a free, full and fast swinging of the clubhead through the ball by the hands, wrists, and arms at the appropriate time during the downswing."

Jack's article, particularly its graphics, offers probably the best advice to be found on a subject in which descriptions are sparse and hard to come by. What there is seems to be provided by champions' descriptions of their own swings in which they say they perceive almost nothing of the actual release of the clubhead. Most describe release simply as a reflex action, so fast that no player can possibly have time to even think of it.

When all is right at the waist, they say that release is the simplest move in golf.

Release is total. Once applied, it carries the clubhead through two-thirds of the combined length of the downswing and follow-through. Release begins with the top assembly at just above waist height. Here, for the first time under their own power, the arms, wrists, and hands deliver the clubhead from its position behind the player, along its locus through the ball, and on to the point where the player's right arm, wrist, and clubshaft form a straight line horizontal to the ground.

Release ends at this point with the clubhead as far

away from the player as it gets throughout the whole of the swing.

This is the position so well documented in hundreds of wonderful photographs of some master golfer or other squinting along his right arm and clubshaft as would a rifleman, though he himself sees no more of the position than he would a passing bullet.

This is effortless release. The power was not turned on (released) until *the straight left arm* (though not the clubshaft) was horizontal to the ground and pointing straight *away* from target, nor consciously turned off until *the straight right arm and clubshaft* were horizontal to the ground and pointing straight *toward* the target, the right forearm's rotation over the left being the reverse of its position in the backswing.

The uncocking right elbow assembly and wrists delivers the clubhead through the ball at maximum speed and with no thought whatsoever of the angle of the clubface, which was taken care of in the preliminaries before the swing began.

Not until a few inches through the ball does the left side of the player's face and left ear tilt upward, the right ear and upper torso holding absolutely steady in their vertical plane.

While releasing their power, the arms have traveled through a complete half circle—180 degrees. They have pulled the clubhead through 270 degrees or more. From start down to impact, the right shoulder has moved through barely 45 degrees.

Available by the thousand to help the poorer golfer are photographs and diagrams of expert players before, at, and through impact. A couple of excellent books of swing sequences published specifically for this purpose are listed among the sources at the back of this book. Any student or determined swing rebuilder would do well to study them closely.

He will discover that an inch through impact the player's straight right arm is at a full 45 degrees to his right shoulder. No matter at which master player he cares to look, from the top of the swing through impact the right shoulder has moved less than a foot, simply returning to the position it occupied at address or very nearly so.

Control of this tiny and relatively easy movement has maximized both the length and the leverage available to the arms, hands, shaft, and clubhead, at the same time providing a constant coordinate and fulcrum (the right shoulder) from which to hit. It is a fulcrum such as this, fixed in its reference, which provides the three qualities so coveted by all long handicap golfers: power, timing and repeatability.

Remember Henry Longhurst's aside to Peter Alliss? "If as we swing we pay more attention to the parts that do not move at all, or move very little, might we not better control the parts that do?"

At this important point the right shoulder joins the right ear and the hips as the three parts which move scarcely at all or only a foot or so until the ball is on its way.

The right shoulder remains well back in this vital position until pulled under the player's head and toward the target as the clubhead swings up into the first stage of follow-through. The swing sequences of Sam Snead and other great players in Bernard Cook's *Golf—A Practical Guide* depict the correct right shoulder movement perfectly, that of Snead being quite remarkable. Knowing where the right shoulder is at address and must be when the hit is made is vital when setting up to play any shot.

Excessive movement of the right shoulder before the hit may force a sway, even a small one. This is perhaps the easiest to detect of the couple of mistakes that can wreck an otherwise perfect swing very late on its correct locus to the ball.

Much is to be learned from the study of photographs of swing sequences or use of the still advance mechanism on the VCR. Another thing of great value to be seen is that these studies are proof positive that all expert players have one thing in common as they strike the ball. It is that despite all personal idiosyncrasies, at the moment of impact, their hands, left armpit, and the fly of the trousers are as near as can be in an exact vertical plane. Naturally, these three points are staggered by just a few inches front to back, but viewed from the front they are in an exact vertical line.

If all aspiring players could find the discipline to emulate this none-too-difficult lineup as they strike the ball, then that change alone would work wonders in the way of timing and power.

Follow-Through

Here's a question that is often asked: Once the ball has left the clubface, does it really matter in what manner or shape the player finishes out his swing? The answer is that it most certainly does.

Just as a classic maypole tells its owner that all was well throughout the swing, difficulties in balance, extension, or arm direction making their appearance in the late stage of release or in the follow-through can be a valuable early warning that all is not well farther back.

With a full understanding of the four elements fundamental to a golf swing and sufficient effort blending them fully into his own, within reason, any player sound in wind and limb and of good attitude should be well able to break 80.

His newfound knowledge, particularly of the correct locus down and through the golf ball, cannot help but present him with the correct loci of the hands and clubhead beyond the ball and into follow-through. No work whatsoever will be required on these, for when all is as it should be in the swing they are preordained.

What is required, if it can be remembered through the joy in ownership of a dependable swing, is to develop a good acquaintance with them. A classic maypole telling its owner that all is well with his swing is not the same thing as the owner having the fullest possible knowledge of the loci that produced the maypole.

A player on the way to losing his edge may detect an off-locus follow-through long before serious problems become apparent on the business side of the ball. Early restoration of the hands and clubhead loci beyond impact may very well limit the damage and even get things completely back on track.

If it does not, the first place to tighten up is on the positioning and immovability of the right ear throughout the stroke.

9

Should It Still Elude You

Many readers long disappointed with the level of their handicaps will have a history of occasional instruction that has failed to impart a clear picture—or any picture at all—of exactly where they must swing the clubhead.

Without a picture, practice is futile, bringing disenchantment and an early return to the spurious comfort of the old ineffective swing the player knows so well and mistakenly believes provides the best game of which he is capable. What the old swing does provide is a clubhead miles off track with the owner unaware of it.

Curiously, a novice having had no instruction at all and knowing nothing of the terminology or mechanics of the stroke will, by cutting across his ball, hit huge slices every bit as well as millions of club members do around their home courses. However, when a passing expert suggests that he might try holding his right ear steady and bring his clubhead to the front at the level of his knee, he quickly produces powerful, well-directed shots, having never heard of weight shift or start down. Unbeknown to him, he is already employing both.

With the priceless gifts of a top anchor to his swing and the true locus of the hitting stroke, our friend has the best possible chance of eventually playing down to single figures. These same gifts will bring similar improvement to any player who determines the position of the clubhead correctly.

With his newfound ability to bring his top assembly to the waist he will say goodbye to the wild men. He will stride right through those whose jerky stringing together of weight transfer, start down, the position at the waist, and commencement of release sees them doing everything right except really hitting the ball.

For years he has been urged to "go out and trust your swing," an instruction guaranteed to produce frustration in all poor players who simply have no swing to trust.

No longer. His only concern is the eradication of all jerkiness as he swings through these positions and the dreamlike references that take his golf club into its horizontal position through the ball. If his sweet swinging encourages him to turn up the wick, so much the better.

It would be easy to end here with the usual good wishes for progress with your rebuild. Easy, but for the certain knowledge that some will encounter continuing difficulty in harnessing weight transfer and the first move down of the hands to their swings. Without continuous encouragement they will succumb as so many have to abandoning weight transfer and with it their very reason for being on the golf course.

This is tragic, for a quitter aware of the correct locus to the ball was so very nearly there!

From remarks made by golfers in explaining their failure to cope with weight transfer, it seems that the standard description of the slide-cum-rotation which covers the movement of the two hips through three quite different positions in something less than a second is a complexity which must have defeated millions.

All that can be done in such cases is to urge perseverance and perhaps to suggest some alternative thinking.

For those unable to make a proper transfer by reference to the hips, there are alternatives that in their case might bring more success. Anything is better than simply to give up. It can sometimes be a help to use the waist, of which there is only one. Bobby Jones recommended this reference that he presented as "a simple unwinding of the trunk."

In the backswing, the hips describe their clockwise turn to the right and without pause initiate the hitting stroke with their slide-cum-rotation to the left. As they do so, the navel follows two very simple loci. The first from the point where it faced the ball at address to somewhere above the inside of the right foot. The second back through the point it occupied at address and on to finish above the inside of the left foot.

This reference is simplicity itself and provides much more benefit than just the proper transfer of weight. It can also help to promote a consistent pivot. It will ensure that transfer always powers the top assembly's move down to the waist and can be a guide to the cocked right elbow as it is lowered into the crucial position just above the belt.

Also worth mentioning once more is the help to be had from the study of photographic swing sequences.

Look very closely at the factor common to all good players as they strike the ball.

At impact it can be clearly seen that the hands, left armpit, and the fly of the trousers are in an exact vertical plane. The straight right arm is at 45 degrees to both the right shoulder and the rubber grip.

This is not a difficult position to emulate, but can only be arrived at following an adequate transfer of the weight. If no transfer or an apology for a transfer is made, the fly of the trousers will lag way behind and the beautiful ZED formed by the shoulders, the right arm, and the clubshaft a foot or so before the hit is made, will disappear as it does with all shots incorrectly played off the back foot.

Practicing this perfect position from which to make the hit will carry the bonus of greatly improved power and timing.

Should satisfactory striking still elude a player, or leave him, the first place to look is his centering. Is there a sway of the head and upper torso to the left? Even a little one? Loss of centering will dismantle the radii and demolish all timing whether the clubhead is held on a correct in-to-out locus or not.

A sway is usually a legacy from the days of turning on the power above the shoulders, a terrible habit not yet eradicated. Less likely, a sway may arrive by means of weight transfer unnecessarily overdone. Whether the cause is old or new the player should remember that it is upper body movement that carries the head to the left and practically never the other way around. Once the torso has begun to sway to the left, no amount of concentration on the right ear will restrain it.

Fortunately, a temporary switch of concentration to holding not the head but the sternum and right side of the upper body in its vertical plane *while releasing from the right shoulder*, can do much to help the player stay well centered and behind the ball.

If quite satisfied that there is no sway, he must ask himself if he is absolutely certain that he knows where the clubhead is coming down its lower locus on the hitting stroke.

Top players continually need to check that their clubhead gets to the rear at a specific point on its backswing locus about shoulder height or very nearly so and exits to the front at knee height or thereabouts on the hitting stroke.

Coming down to just above waist height, the holding of the shaft on its downswing plane and the clubhead to the rear is the function of the set and cock of both the right elbow assembly and wrists. If transfer and start down have been well done and the waist properly arrived at, it is difficult to spoil any shot. Difficult, but not impossible.

If a shot is spoiled this late in an otherwise sound hitting stroke, it is usually done by a small unconscious flip of the hands in their anxiety to hit too early at the ball, instead of smoothly dragging the accelerating clubhead through it.

The flip of the hands may be very small, but the damage is very great. Usually flipped forward just below the belt, the back of the left hand and the palm of the right turn slightly toward the player's front. The right thumb then points straight down a line away from the target and not obliquely upward and to the rear. The right thumb should not point horizontally away to the player's right until the hands are level with the upper right thigh.

A quitting left arm which is not fully firm at impact as it should be, can also spoil an otherwise good-looking downswing late in the stroke.

If undetected, an insidious loss of a good locus so very late in the shot can go on forever—a heartbreak if ever there was one. The ruination of many a promising player and of not a few champion golfers.

The good news is that these annoying lapses occur a foot or so from the player's eyes and once isolated may be cured by use of his own common sense and geometrical reasoning. It requires that the set of the right thumb be held until it points away down the target line at the thigh and not at the waist, which is far too early. If the set of the wrists is firm and there is no involuntary flip of the hands, the left arm will have no need of quitting.

Preliminaries too may need some small adjustment. With cutting across the ball from outside the line now consigned to history, it should be a pleasure to aim for the straight shot or slight draw instead of forever aiming off to counteract a perpetual slice.

The positioning of the ball at address may require slight alteration. It can now be taken a shade farther forward (to the left); a great advantage for which a correct weight transfer is entirely responsible.

Remember, the experts are in agreement that all a player needs to make progress is an understanding that a powerful repeating swing can be built by blending all other facets into and around just four fundamentals. With these in place, all necessary adjustments can be made and further polish applied to improve a swing to its maximum effectiveness. Touring professionals do it all the time.

Sadly, no amount of adjustment will make anything of a swing lacking any one of the four essentials of which transfer of the weight below the waist and a properly powered and directed first move down from the top are considered to be absolutely crucial.

In terms of a correctly struck shot, the waist-high position is the most important coordinate in golf. To repeat once again, not until the upper assembly has been lowered to the waist, or just above it, do the arms and still fully cocked wrists and right elbow release any of their power.

Finally, just a paragraph or two to explain the total absence in these chapters of the short games (plural) and their place in the scheme of things.

When an ambitious player seeks advice on the best way to reduce a handicap of, say, 26, he will invariably be told that the thing most likely to yield him shots lies in sharpening up his "short game." This can be tantamount to cruelty.

His scores reveal that he has broken 100 just four times in three seasons of playing in club competitions. A further season of intensive practice around the greens sees him knocking it in close from 10 yards off with some regularity, but when he does it is still his fourth or fifth shot to the green. His handicap reduces, certainly, but at best he finds himself with a handicap of 22.

In order to improve substantially, a high handicap player simply must find the way to be on or nearly on the greens in regulation 16 or 17 times in every round; to hit his tee shots—when everything is in his favor—reasonably straight and reasonably far and to follow them with a further powerful, well-directed stroke.

It is done all the time by players with a thorough knowledge of the path their clubheads must follow in the hitting stroke and the ability—bought with sheer determination—to apply it. There is no other way.

For many readers the shape of that path should now be reasonably clear. From here on, every stroke must be designed to reduce the huge margin of difference between the correct and the incorrect positions as the clubhead gets to the front. It really is not too difficult to reduce a three-foot discrepancy to one foot in a single evening, bringing with it an early improvement in both length and direction.

Only when the long game is right do the short games acquire major significance in shaving off the strokes to pull a handicap down from, say, nine to three or four surprisingly quickly.

The term "short game" is a blatant misnomer. It lumps together at least four types of shots, each requiring changes of technique that differ considerably. The shortest of these, of course, is the straight-faced iron played very much as a long putt while remembering that it is not a long putt. Another is the little hands and arms shot played with a variety of irons as required and offering the greatest of golfing pleasure when the ball is knocked in really close.

Then there is the very different long run-up, born in Scotland centuries ago and now enjoying belated interest, even popularity, worldwide.

A fourth is the short pitch, which must include the lob, so recently born in the United States of America.

For full measure the greenside bunker shot may well be considered a fifth quite separate short shot, together with a couple more not to be mentioned as the point is already made.

A variety of short games then, calling for differing techniques and a considerable degree of touch and feel, which is simply another name for applied geometrical mathematics.

That the thousands of offerings on mastering the "short game" have had so little measurable effect in reducing players' handicaps is due not so much to the degree of difficulty which these little shots present as lack of knowledge of the makeup of the full shot.

It is the full shots that put the three or four on the card and not the five, six, or seven, thus accounting for the first 18 strokes (at least) of a player's handicap.

A golfer with the knowledge required to bring off the full shot with reasonable accuracy time after time, knows perfectly well why it is that he can do so, though most cannot turn their knowledge into words.

In his all-important practice of the short games, he will study the loci of the little shots even more assiduously, for the path he must make his clubhead follow may be very short indeed, as are his coordinates governing the small movement the hands must make just an inch or two from his lap.

With his understanding of loci and coordinates (though he may never have known them as that) he will have little use for textbooks as he sets about getting up and down successfully from a few feet off the green.

If you attempt to rebuild your swing, keep on. Don't give up. A successful golf swing is acquired not by strength, but by perseverance—by steadily building-in what is known to be correct and by steadily eliminating what is known to be incorrect. There is no other way.

Good luck to all who may find any part of this review of the teaching of the old masters helpful in improving it.

Sources

Peter Alliss: An Autobiography. Collins 1981, by kind permission of Peter Alliss.

Bobby Jones on Golf by Bobby Jones. Cassell & Co Ltd. 1968. © Jonesheirs Inc. Reprinted by kind permission of the family of Robert T. Jones Jr. Via the good offices of Alston and Bird L.L.P., 1201 West Peachtree St, Atlanta, GA U.S.A.

Harvey Penick's Little Green Golf Book by Harvey Penick. © Harvey Penick, Bud Shrake, and Helen Penick 1994. By kind permission of Harper Collins Publishers Ltd.

And If You Play Golf You're My Friend by Harvey Penick. © Harvey Penick, Bud Shrake and Helen Penick 1993. Reprinted with the permission of Simon & Schuster, Adult Publishing Group, New York, NY 10020 U.S.A.

How to Play Your Best Golf All the Time by Tommy Armour. © 1954 Reproduced by kind permission of Hodder & Stoughton Ltd.; Reprinted with the permission of Simon & Schuster, Adult Publishing Group, New York, NY 10020 U.S.A.

Five Lessons: The Modern Fundamentals of Golf by Ben Hogan with H. Warren Wind. Drawings by Anthony Ravielli. Nicholas Kaye Ltd. 1957. Pan Books 1988. Extracts © Reproduced by kind permission of the heirs of Ben Hogan. Via the good offices of Kelly, Hart & Hallman, A.A.L., Main Street, Fort Worth, TX U.S.A.

Golf—A Practical Guide by Bernard Cooke. Read International Books Ltd. 1987, 1993.

The P.G.A. European Guide to Better Golf by Mark Wilson. Tech Advisor, Tommy Horton; Photos, Phil Sheldon. Pan Books 1986.

Jacklin's Golf Secrets by Tony Jacklin and Peter Dobereiner. Stanley Paul and Co Ltd. 1983.

"Drive for Show—Putt for Dough" by Greg Norman. Golf School 1997 by kind permission of *Golf Monthly* Magazine.

"A Key to Releasing" by Jack Nicklaus with Ken Bowden. Golf School 1997 by kind permission of *Golf Monthly* Magazine.

"The Right Shin Post" by Mr X. © 1966 by kind permission of *Golf Monthly* Magazine.

"Weight Transfer" by Mike Mural Jr. *PGA Magazine* (U.S.A.) 1983. Reproduced by *Golf Monthly* Magazine 1983. By kind permission of The Professional Golfers Association of America.